INSIDE-OUT CHRISTIANITY

A Study of Colossians by

FLORENCE O. COLLINS

20th century christian

2809 Granny White Pike
Nashville, TN 37204

INSIDE-OUT
CHRISTIANITY

A Study of Colossians by
FLORENCE O. COLLINS

In Memory of
Clinton
an intelligent, honest, gentle son

Acknowledgments

The much-needed help in preparing this book consumed an abundance of time and thought of those persons who so freely and efficiently gave it to me. I deeply thank them all. They are:

Williams C. Collins, our son, and Jo Ann McCool, who each typed an early manuscript;

G. Clinton Collins, III, our son, who corrected the syntax of many drafts;

Joanna O. Long, writing instructor, who carefully critiqued the entire manuscript and advised and encouraged me;

J. Cliett Goodpasture, Robert J. Niebel, Sr., and Michelle Burke, the knowledgeable and courteous publishing staff of Twentieth Century Christian;

Many Bible teachers and pupils who shared their knowledge with me;

Many friends who prayed for me;

Harold L. and Verna S. Olmstead, my parents, who taught me to trust;

George C. Collins, Jr., my husband, who supported me in every way;

My heavenly Father, who is preparing me.

Contents

Chapter 1

Colossians 1:1-2

God loves everybody and wants each person to have a life which is full, mature and strong. These are qualities of eternal life, in addition to its being unending. By knowing Him and His Son, Jesus Christ, we can possess this life (John 17:3). Knowing about Him from His Word, the Bible, is the first step toward truly knowing Him.

The book of Colossians is not about a system of religion and its rituals. It is not just a rule book for daily living. It is not a psychoanalysis of the human race. Like all the books of the Bible, it is the revelation of God through a Person—the Lord Jesus Christ. It tells who He is, what He has done, what He is doing and will do. Nowhere else do we find a deeper or more concise exposition of the Son of God than in Colossians.

This letter makes wonderful promises to those who trust themselves to Jesus Christ. It tells how He made it possible for them to have fellowship with God. It tells how Christ is *in* believers and they are *in* Him. It tells how He is their hope of glory and how believers are changed as they become the kind of people God wants them to be.

Colossians also gently but soundly warns us of the consequences of false worship and wrong dealings with others. It tells God's plan for the universe and the fulfillment of this plan through Jesus Christ.

From the book of Colossians, we learn much about the nature of the church. We pray that each reader will truly believe what God has revealed about Himself and His church in this book.

Background Information

The writer of Colossians was the apostle Paul. He wrote to a congregation of Christians in the town of Colosse in the country now known as Turkey. This letter was also to be read by the church in Laodicea (4:16).

At the time Paul wrote this letter, he was a prisoner of the Roman government. He didn't personally know the congregation at Colosse but had heard of them, most likely from Epaphras, one of their members who was with Paul at this time (1:4; 4:12-13).

Throughout the book, we see Paul's love for the Colossian Christians and his concern for their spiritual safety, which was endangered by false teaching being introduced to them. False teaching was not peculiar to those times, nor to us today.

From what is described of this particular heresy, we may deduce it came through at least two channels: Judaism and gnosticism (2:8, 16-18). "No one knows exactly what this philosophy was. It is enough to know that it was not after Christ."[1] Any religion which doesn't give the honor to Jesus Christ that God gives Him is false. Any person who wants to have a relationship with the God of heaven and earth must approach Him through Jesus only (John 14:6).

Judaistic teachers were trying to get Christians to practice rituals of the Mosaic law, including abstinence from certain foods and drinks and observance of special days (2:16-17). Angel worship had also crept into orthodox Jewish religion and was being practiced by some. The law of Moses was good and achieved the purpose for which God gave it, which was to bring people to Christ (Galatians 3:24). But trusting it to save is hopeless. No one is justified before God by law. It is only by faith in Christ that we can become righteous (Galatians 3:11).

Gnosticism was a philosophy which originated with Satan and was bred in people's imagination. Therefore it was based on falsehood. Gnostics believed that all matter is essentially evil and that spirit is holy. Therefore, in their minds, since God is a spirit, He was far removed from the creation and maintenance of matter. They devised the theory that creation was accomplished as a result of many emanations, or outflows, from God through angelic beings. Supposedly, each outflow was further removed from God, therefore less

12

holy, and its ruling "spirits" of lesser rank than those of previous ones. After innumerable emanations there was one far enough removed from God and so unholy that evil matter, including the human body, could be created. This doctrine that the human body is evil attacked the very foundation of Christian faith: the fact that Jesus Christ is God Himself in human form (Philippians 2:8).

Any theory which denies the direct creation of mankind by God, whether it teaches that human life has become of a higher level than original human life or of a lower level through the ages, is false. The human race was created by God in God's image and likeness (Genesis 1:26-27). According to the Gnostics, the human body, composed of evil matter, holds the spirit of man prisoner. They also claim that the human race is subject to myriad mystical beings. This belief makes mankind less than human, for it denies that he is a responsible creature.

Gnostics believed they could never be free from evil until they were freed from their bodies. Some adherents punished and neglected their own bodies, trying to rid themselves of evil. Others hopelessly abandoned the desire to be better and lived in unrestricted sin. Gnostics thought that salvation was possible, but only through what they knew. Since some were considered to know more than others, we can see that gnosticism was a philosophy of exclusion and separation: separation of the intellectual from the ignorant; of God from creation; of man's spirit from his body. Only in Christ can all things hold together (1:17).

The hope of gnosticism was in what a person *knew*. The hope of Judaism was in what a person *did*. The hope of Christianity is in a *Person* and what *He* did! The hope of Christianity is not a fantasy, but a fact (1:5, 23).[2]

False doctrines are not just a thing of the past. All false religions contain one or both of these two elements: faith in what humans know, and faith in what humans can do. If our faith is in our own behavior, in religious leaders with so-called "special" powers, or in looking into and worshiping our own souls and intellect, we will live in a smaller spiritual world than God offers us. If we hold the fatalistic view that we are being helplessly influenced by some part of the physical universe, such as a planet, or by supernatural powers, we cannot attain the maturity God planned for us.

When Paul wrote this letter, the Colossian Christians' faith had not yet been undermined by the false teaching they'd been exposed to. But Paul, knowing the power of Satan, warned them before they reached the "point of no return."

It is possible for any Christian to reach that point. Listening to and following false teaching is as spiritually hazardous as outer space travel is physically dangerous. Astronauts have entered that unnatural environment—from first spending only a few minutes in space to now living there for weeks. Today space "walkers" venture farther and are safe only when tethered to their spaceship by a strong lifeline.

In the spiritual realm, Christians have no promise of being safe if they repeatedly choose to live in the unnatural environment ruled by Satan. With alluring philosophies and adventures, he beckons us from the call of God's Word. Some are tempted to believe him. If we continue to be guided by Satan, he will lead us into the predicament of holding to Christ by only a thread. Perhaps it is the thread of seldom worshiping with other Christians, of rarely reading the Bible, or of praying only when in need. The thread may be weakened by mistakenly assuming that our present faith is as valid as the belief we once had, or it may be a "secondhand" faith we have tried to borrow from our family's traditional faith. Even while hanging by a thread, we can be unaware of our peril. Then with one more gibe at God's Word, Satan calls us. Almost without knowing it, we may turn the thread loose and never again be able to repent (Hebrews 6:4-6).

But we will be secure as long as we hold Christ's hand. We can foolishly run away from Him, but no one, not even the devil himself, can *snatch* us from God's hand (John 10:27-29).

Jesus Christ alone is sufficient for every need. True Christianity is not a "Christ-plus" religion. Regardless of what name it is known by, even "Christian," a religion that interposes anything or anyone except Jesus Christ between individuals and God is false and therefore futile.

The book of Colossians speaks much of "Christ in you" and of being "in Christ." This relationship is a wonderful privilege. Let each one of us determine within his own soul to allow himself to be surrounded by Christ and to be permeated by Him from within.

Many scriptures will be referred to in the lessons, and it will help make the meaning clearer if you read these references. The entire passage covered in each section will appear at the beginning of that section. Each of these quotations is from the New King James Version. Read this passage before studying that part of the lesson, and keep your Bible open so you can refer to it often. You should begin each study period with prayer, asking God, through His Spirit, to give you understanding.

Before continuing your study, you should read all of the short book of Colossians. As you read, if you pay close attention to the number of times Christ is mentioned, you will understand the central theme of the book. It will be helpful if you list what is said about Christ each time He is mentioned. You should have a total of at least thirty-three items.

Salutation
Colossians 1:1-2

Paul, an apostle of Jesus Christ by the will of God, and Timothy our brother, To the saints and faithful brethren in Christ who are in Colosse: Grace to you and peace from God our Father and the Lord Jesus Christ.

As was the custom of his day, Paul signed his letter at the beginning. He told what his office was—that is, that he was an apostle, meaning that he was a messenger chosen to deliver a certain message and sent with the authority of the One who sent him. Next he named the Sender: Jesus Christ. Before he was converted, Paul had seen Christ on the road to Damascus, and he had been taught by Him in the desert (Acts 9:3-5; Galatians 1:16-17). He was sent with the same authority as the original eleven apostles (Mark 16:14-15). Paul was an apostle not merely because he had the backing of a church, but "by the will of God" Himself. He included Timothy, who was with him at the time, in the signature.

15

The name *Jesus* does not appear in the whole book without the title "Christ" or "Lord." The name *Jesus* means "savior," and certainly we are glad He is that. But the title *Christ* means "the anointed One" and refers to the one prophesied to be king. That One was to be the eternal Son of God (Psalm 2:7; Hebrews 1:5). The word *lord* means "master." By emphasizing His Sonship and lordship, Paul is pointing out that Jesus was God Himself in a human body.

Paul addressed this letter to the saints at Colosse. The word *saint* means "one separated, or set apart for a specific use." A Christian saint is separated for God's use, not separated from or above other Christians. All believers are called "saints" in the Bible. Paul also called the Colossian Christians his "faithful brothers." They were brothers because they were in Christ just as he was in Christ. If we are in Christ, we too are brothers and sisters of Paul, who wrote a large part of the New Testament.

We would begin a letter with some endearing term. Paul began his with a much more meaningful expression of his love—he wished them grace and peace. Christians who were being bombarded with speculative doctrine, and who may have seen those they loved believing this teaching, needed peace. If non-Christians chanced to read this letter, they were separated from God and needed peace with God.

But before peace can come to any of us, we must accept grace. Grace is the *undeserved* favor of God with all that it includes. Paul states his desires for them in the correct order; grace precedes peace. One may have a false sense of security based on man-made theories, but a person can have real peace only through receiving the grace of God made possible through the cross.

Paul called God "*our* Father." He is the father of all who believe in and obey His Son, and He puts them in His family together. How much better to be united than to be separated by a divisive philosophy!

Questions

The questions following each chapter are designed to help you organize your thinking on the teachings of the letter to the Colossians and applying them in your life. I hope that you will prayerfully answer them.

1. What is Christian maturity? What other kinds of maturity are there? Write a description of Christian maturity and file it until you complete your study of Colossians.
2. What is the first criterion for judging a doctrine (2:8)?
3. In what instances has Christian fellowship helped you, or would have helped you had it been present?
4. Can grace be earned? Can salvation be earned?

Chapter 2

Colossians 1:3-12

In this portion of the book Paul tells the Christians at Colosse how he prays for them. Knowing this apostle had solicited the power of God on their behalf surely must have encouraged them. When a Christian friend says, "I'm praying for you," you can know that all the forces of heaven are standing at attention ready to come to your service.

Paul's prayer is in several parts. First, he tells the things for which he gives thanks (1:3-8); next, he petitions God for the Colossians' needs (1:9-11). Then it seems that Paul becomes so enthralled by Jesus Christ that his prayer erupts into a recounting of Christ's glorious attributes. This illustrious summary includes Christ's position in relation to God and to man, and His work in heaven and on earth (1:12-23).

As we study Paul's prayer, we notice the importance of certain words: faith, love, hope, truth, knowledge. In these verses are two concepts which are important throughout the book. They are expressed by the words "in Christ" and "filled" or "fullness." Life in Christ is described as being all-encompassing. No one is left out; no area of a believer's life is slighted. Jesus has done the same for the simpleminded that He has done for the super-intelligent. His life excludes no one and has no limits, if we continue to have faith in Him.

We read here that Colossian Christians had love for *all* the saints; that the Gospel was bearing fruit *all over* the world; and that it is possible for Christians to have *all* (every kind of) spiritual understanding and to please Him in *every* way because they are strengthened with *all* power.

The Christians of Paul's day knew the importance of communicating with each other even when thousands of miles apart. There was no postal service, telephone, radio or satellites, yet they carried news to each other by letter and word of mouth. To them, it was imperative to tell and hear expressions of God's love.

Prayer of Thanksgiving for the Colossian Christians
Colossians 1:3-8

We give thanks to the God and Father of our Lord Jesus Christ, praying always for you, since we heard of your faith in Christ Jesus and of your love for all the saints; because of the hope which is laid up for you in heaven, of which you heard before in the word of the truth of the gospel, which has come to you, as it has also in all the world, and is bringing forth fruit, as it is also among you since the day you heard and knew the grace of God in truth; as you also learned from Epaphras, our dear fellow servant, who is a faithful minister of Christ on your behalf, who also declared to us your love in the Spirit.

We would better know what to ask for if all prayers began with thanksgiving, as this one begins. Paul says that he and Timothy are constant in their prayers for the Colossian Christians (1:3, 9). He prays to "God the Father of our Lord Jesus Christ." Some versions of the Bible inaccurately take that phrase from the Greek language in which it was written and translate it as, "We give thanks to God *and* the Father of our Lord Jesus Christ." That translation could leave the false impression that God and the father of Jesus are two different personages. The correct translation is copied above. In this one statement Paul says the holy God Himself fathered a human being, made of so-called "evil" matter, thus affirming the deity of Jesus.

One of the things for which Paul expresses thanks is the hope which is laid up in heaven for believers (1:5). In biblical language the word *hope* never means a doubtful wish.

It refers to a thing which is both desired and confidently expected. Faithful Christians have a "sure and steadfast" hope. This hope is stored up for them in heaven. The compound verb *stored up* means "to be reserved for one, awaiting him."[1]

That which is reserved for us has not been established by human government, nor guaranteed by gold. It has been founded by the God of heaven, Himself, and insured by Christ's entrance into God's presence, made possible by the offering of His own blood (Hebrews 6:18-20).

Paul knew the Colossian Christians had a sure hope because he had heard of their faith in Christ Jesus. False teachers were attempting to undermine that faith. The problem of being exposed to false teaching could be met and solved by the Colossians (and by us today) only by getting back to faith in the person of Christ.

Faith in Jesus Christ Himself is basic to everything else in life. We are like the child who wasn't allowed to drink anything for ten hours before surgery. When he asked for water, hoping to ease his distress, his mother said, "See that bag of fluid hanging beside your bed and dripping into your arm? That will keep you from being thirsty." The child insisted, "But I *am* thirsty! I can't swallow that water." Applying stopgap activities, no matter how pious and noble they may be, to a thirsty soul can only produce a dried-out existence.

If one's spiritual life is disappointing or a failure, it cannot be made right by a few repairs in philosophy or behavior. To have a satisfying, complete life, we must daily and resolutely partake of Jesus Christ, the Source of life.

The expression "in Christ" in verses 2 and 4 elsewhere in the book denotes the place where a Christian's faith resides. It rests in Christ. It is where true Christians live regardless of where circumstances may take them. With an anchor of hope in heaven and a dwelling place in Christ on earth, Christians have every reason to be joyful and fulfilled.

The Colossians' hope inspired in them a love for all the saints. A question which tests the value of one's spiritual life is, "Do I love all the saints?" For the Colossians, faith and hope resulted in the kind of love that is self-sacrificing. That kind of love comes only from God (1 John 4:7). If love isn't present, it is an indication that one is not in the right relationship with God, the Source of love.

The Colossians had faith in our Lord Jesus Christ because they had heard and *accepted* the word of the truth of the Gospel (1:5). The biblical definition of the Gospel is the fact that "Christ died for our sins according to the Scriptures, and that He was buried, and that He rose again the third day according to the Scriptures" (1 Corinthians 15:3-4). The "Word of truth" is based on Christ's death, burial and resurrection.

This event has been proved by both biblical and secular history. It is not a speculation based on human imagination, neither is it a feeling one may have. If it were anything but fact, the Gospel would not be the "Word of truth."

Religions which are not based on truth have no foundation, and regardless of how strong they may seem, they fail to give lasting support to followers. The question is: Do we really *believe* the facts of the Gospel? God gave us the freedom to choose where we put our trust. But no one, not even God, can force another to believe any fact, whether it be of little or of great importance.

Sincere belief is not easy. It means renouncing self and having complete reliance on God (Luke 9:23). Trusting in the good news that Christ died for our sins, was buried and arose from the grave gives us God's forgiveness and power to endure the frustrations, temptations and sufferings of life.

When the Colossians heard the Word of truth they also understood the grace of God in all its truth (1:5-6). One truth about the grace of God is that it was expensive. It cost God His most valuable, most loved Person—His only begotten Son. Another truth about God's grace is that it cannot be purchased. "The gift of God is eternal life in Christ Jesus."

When our oldest son was six years old we told him that soon he would have another little brother. Not able to remember having been without a brother, he asked, "How can I get another brother?" Joking, his father replied, "We'll buy a baby." Clinton scoffed, "Oh, Daddy! Babies come from God. God doesn't sell things—He gives them away." Clinton was beginning to understand the grace of God.

God's grace cannot be earned. "All our righteousnesses are like filthy rags," so "doing our best" is not good enough. Is there any Christian who always does his best? An entire life of gratitude doesn't begin to counterbalance the weight of our debt to God.

The natural result of such a life-giving thing as the Gospel is fruit. This is what happened in Colosse. When a Christian or a body of Christians allows the Holy Spirit to produce His fruit in them, they are ready to increase in numbers, knowledge and good works (1:6). The Spirit of God inspired the writing of God's truth. Therefore He will not oppose that Word, but will be the energizing force that carries it out. The more we know and trust the Bible, the more able we will be to detect lying spirits.

In verse 7, Paul puts his apostolic approval on Epaphras and his teaching. It was probably he who brought the Gospel to Colosse. He had also told Paul of the love they had for him (1:8). "The Spirit is the ruling element of the Colossians' love. 'Love-in-the-Spirit' forms a single compound phrase (in the original)."[2] Christian love cannot be separated from the Holy Spirit because love is a fruit of the Spirit (Galatians 5:22).

Petitions for Colossian Christians
Colossians 1:9-12

For this reason we also, since the day we heard it, do not cease to pray for you, and to ask that you may be filled with the knowledge of His will in all wisdom and spiritual understanding; that you may walk worthy of the Lord, fully pleasing Him, being fruitful in every good work and increasing in the knowledge of God; strengthened with all might, according to His glorious power, for all patience and longsuffering with joy; giving thanks to the Father who has qualified us to be partakers of the inheritance of the saints in the light.

In the petition part of Paul's prayer, he doesn't ask for material blessings for the Colossian Christians or for physical health. He sees that their greatest need at this time is to be filled with the knowledge of God's will. The word translated "knowledge" here refers to a full, intimate knowledge, not just an accumulation of information. His prayer was for a complete knowledge "in all (every kind of) spiritual wisdom and understanding." Human wisdom is of no value toward having real insight into the will of God (1 Corinthians 2:11-14).

The word translated "fill" or "fullness" expresses a concept which could be described as "crammed," "made replete" or "complete." This concept has been illustrated by the following story:

> A chemistry teacher showed his class a beaker holding pebbles to the top. He asked, "Is the beaker full?" A few students were doubtful; so he shook the beaker and added some more pebbles. Then he asked the question again. This time the entire class was satisfied the beaker was full. Then the teacher filled a pitcher with water and poured it over the pebbles until the beaker overflowed. He asked again, "Is the beaker full?" The students hesitantly agreed it was full. Then the teacher poured the water from the beaker, added a tumbler full of salt to it, and poured it back into the beaker. To the beaker which had been described as full, there had been added a quart of water and a tumbler of salt. The experiment could have been carried at least one more step by forcing gas into the beaker.[3]

There are no limits to our infinite God and how He can fill us if we allow Him to do so.

Verse 10 tells the purpose of having such spiritual knowledge—that this knowledge would have an effect on the lives of the Colossian Christians. A heart that is full of the knowledge of God's will overflows into a life of obedience to that will. "The foundation of all Christian character and conduct is laid in the knowledge of the will of God. What it concerns us to know is no abstract truth, or a revelation of a speculative thought, but God's will. He does not show Himself to us merely that we may know, but in order that, knowing, we may do, and what is more than either knowing or doing, in order that we may *be*."[4]

The Bible is a guide for our behavior, for it is God's will revealed in words. We cannot fully know God unless we obey Him. Each time we obey Him we learn more of His nature and love Him more.

The expression "live a life worthy" in verse 10 of the New International Version does not mean that we could ever deserve God's goodness. In the original Greek language, the word translated "worthy" means "suitably" or "appropriately." People who have had their sins forgiven and have a hope laid up for them in heaven are obligated to conduct their lives in a way that demonstrates their gratitude to the One who did this for them. The obligation is not easy to fulfill, but it is possible because they have been "strengthened with *all* power according to *His* glorious might." Only God's power can carry out God's will, and He has given Christians that power through the Holy Spirit who is in them.

It is not enough that Paul prays for these Christians to increase in the knowledge of God's will. Indeed, he also prays that they will increase in the knowledge of God Himself (1:10). The person who has known God's will and been subject to it will learn to know God in the same way a husband and wife know each other. That person is the one who, when he doesn't find a "thou shalt" or "thou shalt not" in the Bible, can still know his Lord's will because he has been living with Him.

Living this kind of life in Christ will help one to reach a goal of endurance, even to the extent of undergoing trials with joy (1:11). There is no promise that Christians will escape adversity. All lives are tried, but life in Christ can be lived with joy. Those who don't know Christ have no promise of being able to rise above despair.

Christian joy is not merely a shallow feeling of pleasure. It is being filled with a profound sense of gladness, well-being and glorious anticipation; it is the result of being aware of

God's constant love. Such joy should not be taken for granted. Thus, Paul prays that the Colossians will be thankful to the Father for giving them this power of endurance with joy. The next two chapters tell how this joy was made possible. They also discuss "the inheritance of the saints."

Questions

1. Why does beginning a prayer with praise and thanksgiving help Christians make the best petitions?
2. What is the connection between truth and faith? Between faith and hope?
3. Whom should Christians not love?
4. Do you deserve God's love?
5. Does your supply of love run low (1 John 4:7-8)?
6. What should be the result of wisdom (1:9-10)?

Chapter 3

Colossians 1:9-23

The false teaching at Colosse was impractical, divisive, and perilous. Yet Paul, in counteracting it, did not take each false tenet, describe it in full and expose its untruth. He was dedicated to telling the *good* news about Jesus Christ. He wrote to the Colossians about the foundation of true religion—the person of Jesus Christ. "The place that Christ holds in any religious teaching determines whether it is true or false."[1] And the place that Christ holds in any heart determines whether that heart is acceptable to God.

Who Christ Is and What He Has Done
Colossians 1:9-23

For this reason we also, since the day we heard it, do not cease to pray for you, and to ask that you may be filled with the knowledge of His will in all wisdom and spiritual understanding; that you may walk worthy of the Lord, fully pleasing Him, being fruitful in every good work and increasing in the knowledge of God; strengthened with all might, according to His glorious power, for all patience and longsuffering with joy; giving thanks to the Father who has qualified us to be partakers of the inheritance of the saints in the light. He has delivered us from the power of darkness and conveyed us into the kingdom of the Son of His love, in whom we have redemption through His blood, the forgiveness of sins. He is the image of the invisible God, the firstborn over all creation. For by Him all things were created that are in heaven and that are on earth, visible and invisible, whether thrones or dominions or principalities or powers. All things were created through Him and for Him. And He is before all things, and in Him all things consist. And He is the head of the body, the church, who is the beginning, the firstborn from the dead, that in all things He may have the preeminence.

For it pleased the Father that in Him all the fullness should dwell, and by Him to reconcile all things to Himself, by Him, whether things on earth or things in heaven, having made peace through the blood of His cross. And you, who once were alienated and enemies in your mind by wicked works, yet now He has reconciled in the body of His flesh through death, to present you holy, and blameless, and above reproach in His sight—if indeed you continue in the faith, grounded and steadfast, and are not moved away from the hope of the gospel which you heard, which was preached to every creature under heaven, of which I, Paul, became a minister.

This passage will be dealt with in two chapters. It tells who Christ is and what God has done through Him. He could do these things only because of who He is. This chapter will discuss who Jesus is: His relationship to God, to the universe, to the human race and to the church. The next chapter will be about what has been done through and by Him.

The pronouns *He* and *Him* when referring to Christ are in the "emphatic" form. They could be translated "He, Himself." Christ, and only Christ, is all-sufficient. He needs no assistance from men or angels. Rather, all need Him. Later in the book we will see additional things that Christ is.

In these verses we find the following:

He is a king (1:13).
He is God's Son and the object of God's love (1:13).
He is the image of God (1:15).
He is the firstborn of all creation (1:15).
He is before all things (1:17).
He is the head of the body, the church (1:18).
He is the beginning (1:18).
He is the firstborn from among the dead (1:18).
He is supreme (1:18).
He is indwelt by all the fullness (1:19).
He is a person (1:22).

Following is a list of the things that have been done through, in and by Christ, in both the physical and spiritual realms:

Believers are made competent to be partakers of the inheritance of the saints in the light (1:12).
Believers have been rescued from the power of darkness (1:13).
Believers have been translated into the kingdom of Christ (1:13).
Believers have been given redemption, the forgiveness of their sins (1:14).
All things have been created by Him (1:16).
All things have been created for Him (1:16).
All things hold together in Him (1:17).
All things are reconciled to God. Peace with God has been made (1:20).
Former enemies of God have been reconciled to God (1:21-22).
Believers can be presented to God holy, without blemish or accusation (1:22).

The last ten statements will be studied in the next chapter.

Look at this life! Is not the life of Jesus far superior to any other? In these twelve verses we can see that He is the source of life and victory in any time, any situation. He gives the power of His life to all who receive Him (1 John 5:11-12).

Who Jesus Is

He is a king (1:13).

When the Bible refers to the "kingdom of God" or the "kingdom of Christ," the Greek word translated "kingdom" alludes to the *rule* of God or of Christ rather than to those over whom He rules. "The scripture 'Repent ye for the kingdom of heaven is at hand' means 'for the rule of God among men impends' rather than that some organization is about to appear."[2]

Today we sometimes are governed by external forces without even being aware of their influence. We schedule meals and bedtime by television news times. We follow the decree of the fashion establishment in the clothes we wear. Some even choose lifestyles according to the example of popular, publicized people. A deliberate, repeated decision is necessary if we want to remain under the rule of Jesus. His commandments are not burdensome (1 John 5:3).

Christ's kingdom is one of light, and there is as much difference between it and the "kingdom of darkness" as there is between physical light and darkness. Darkness brings about illusion, ignorance and fear. It inhibits, enslaves and hides truth. Light promotes growth, helps satisfy our aesthetic need for beauty and improves judgment. It exposes things as they really are, giving knowledge and freedom. The kingdom of darkness is lawless, while Christ's kingdom is governed by the moral law of love.

He is God's Son and the object of His Father's love (1:13).

If nothing else were known of Jesus Christ except that He is God's only begotten Son, that would be enough to command our faith in Him. His standing is far above angels or any other human (Hebrews 1:5). At His baptism and at His transfiguration a voice came out of heaven saying, "This is my beloved Son, in whom I am well pleased." If He is dear to the Almighty God of heaven and earth, surely He should be dear to us!

He is the image of God (1:15).

Christ is not an imitation or reflection of God, or a sort of "junior" God. He is God. The likeness of the head of a king cast into a coin was called an image. An image, as used here, derived its characteristics from the thing it represented. "The likeness, however, is not mere resemblance; rather, it means a deliberate, planned representation. The word translated 'image' also has the meaning of 'manifestation,' especially of that which is hidden, as is emphasized by the words 'the invisible God.'"[3] Jesus said, "He who has seen me has seen the Father" (John 14:9). Hebrews 1:3 says that Christ is the very image of God's substance. The use of the word *substance* tells us that the very essence of God existed and was expressed in His Son.[4] God wants everyone to know Him, so He sent His Son as the final revelation of Himself in a form that could be understood by mankind. The only way one can know God is to know Jesus Christ.

He is the firstborn over all creation (1:15).

The term *firstborn* here does not mean He was first as to the time of His birth. It refers to His position. His position in relation to all creation is the same as that of the Hebrew firstborn son to all other children in the family. Under the law of Moses the firstborn son inherited a double portion of his father's possessions.

The oldest son usually succeeded his father to the throne. "Primogeniture (the inheritance rights of the eldest son) in the early ages carried with it the rights of full heirship, involving representation of the father both in his religious and civil capacity, and sovereignty within the house."[5] Therefore, this term means that the position of the firstborn bestowed not only honor, but responsibility.

One responsibility of the firstborn Israelite sons was that they be set apart as an offering for God. This was in memory of the time when the firstborn sons had not been killed when they left Egypt. The Israelites had believed God when He said He would accept the blood of a Passover lamb in place of the life of their firstborn if they placed the blood on the doorposts and lintels of their homes (Exodus 12:1-14; 13:11-15). God required that the ordinance of the offering of the firstborn continue to be observed after the Israelites reached Canaan. But God allowed a substitute offering to be made (Numbers 3:11-12; 41-51). Israelite firstborn sons were redeemed by that substitute, and not one was sacrificed.

31

But the firstborn Son of creation was not redeemed by a substitute. He, Himself, became our Passover Lamb and was sacrificed on the cross (1 Corinthians 5:7). Thus He fulfilled His responsibility as firstborn.

One day He will receive the inheritance and honor due Him as firstborn of all creation. That will be the day when every creature in heaven and earth will bless Him as their Passover Lamb and give Him glory and dominion (Revelation 5:8-14).

He is before all things (1:17).

The use of the present tense of the verb "is" has meaning for us. This usage shows the pre-existent aspect of Christ's eternal life. When speaking to the Pharisees Jesus said, "Before Abraham was, I AM" (John 8:58). He did not say, "Before Abraham was, I was." He applied to Himself the sacred name of God which denotes eternity—the name "I Am" (Exodus 3:13-14).

The three following attributes of Christ pertain to His relationship to His new creation, the church:

He is the head of the body, the church (1:18).

The church is not a body in the same way we consider a club, political party or any other organization a body. It is a body like the human body which has a head and many members such as eyes, muscles and feet. Its members are functional parts of this living organism. "The church is His (Christ's) idea, not ours. It is His body, not ours."[6] Just as Eve was taken from Adam's side, the church which is called the "bride of Christ" is the extension of Christ in the world. It is composed of those whom God has called out of the world, have responded to His call, and have been placed there by Him. "Just as we think our thoughts and then express them to the external world through our bodies, so the church, the body of Christ, is to express Christ to the world."[7]

Christ's body receives its life from Him and ideally is controlled by Him. When members don't submit they weaken the church, just as a severed nerve in a physical body causes loss of function in one or more members. When all members avail themselves of direct contact with the head, there is health and vigor in the church.

He is the beginning (1:18).

The word translated "beginning" means "the active cause" or "origin." Just as the physical universe received its life through Christ, so the new spiritual creation, the church, receives its life from Him.

He is the firstborn from among the dead (1:18).

As we have seen, Christ by his inherent nature has always been the firstborn of creation. He now has this exalted position in relation to the church, His spiritual creation. This position was not the result of His life, but of His death. He alone is "the firstborn out from among the dead" and has been declared the Son of God with power because of His resurrection (Romans 1:4). Of all who have lived on earth, He is the first and only one to die, live again and never again die (Romans 6:9).

He has the supremacy in all things (1:18).

"Literally, this passage reads, 'that He might become the first,' or 'might take first place.' The thought of 'becoming' as distinguished from 'being' must not be lost."[8] In this verse we see that He attained this most superior rank through His resurrection. He has now returned to heaven and is seated at God's right hand and will remain there until His enemies are the footstool of His feet (Hebrews 1:3, 13).

He is indwelt by the fullness (1:19).

The word *dwell* means "to be permanently at home." The word *fullness* is modified by the word *all*, which leads us to think it applies to a maximum of fullness. The word translated "fullness" here was used in Paul's day to describe a ship which was completely equipped with all the crew, supplies, cargo, or artillery and ammunition that would be needed to complete a voyage. This means that Jesus is lacking in nothing, but can supply every need.

The illustration of fullness given in chapter 2 is restricted by what man has discovered. The Father's ways are so high above our ways that we must not let our thinking be limited by man's incomplete knowledge, but be open to every possible dimension of God's truth, and believe it because He stated it. Believing God's truth enough to decide to obey it precedes understanding it (John 7:17).

He is a person (1:22).

This verse tells us that it was by Christ's physical body that He reconciled believers to God. God had given His people the rituals of animal sacrifices so they could be called clean (Leviticus 16). But the blood of bulls and goats never *took away* sins or cleansed anyone's conscience (Hebrews 9:13-14; 10:4). No animal or angelic being could satisfy the holiness of God. It was necessary that the penalty for the sins of the human race be paid by a perfect human. Jesus Christ was that person. Although He is a king, although He is dear to His Father and is the image of God, although He is the firstborn of creation, it was necessary that He become a human being so He could "bear our sins in His own body on the tree" (1 Peter 2:24). God "laid on Him the iniquity of us all." If we refuse His sacrifice on our behalf we must bear the guilt of our own sins and can never be presented to God "holy, without blemish and free from accusation." God has said, "Be holy, for I am holy" (Leviticus 19:2; 1 Peter 1:16). God's holiness is incomprehensible to mankind. By learning of the holiness of God, we can know the sinfulness of sin. Then we can have the contrite heart which God forgives.

In the next chapter, we will study what was done through and by Christ.

Questions
1. Why is it important to know Christ (John 1:18)?
2. Which four books of the New Testament show what Christ is like?
3. As what part of the body of Christ are you willing to be placed by God (1 Corinthians 12:18)?
4. What does Christ's resurrection mean to you (1 Corinthians 15:13-14; Romans 6:4, 20-22)?
5. How would you describe Jesus Christ's power and personality?
6. How does knowledge of God's holiness expose the sinfulness of sin (Genesis 1:27; 3:6-7; John 1:18)?

Chapter 4

Colossians 1:9-23

We now look more deeply into what God has done through Christ. He has done these things on behalf of mankind and all creation. They could not have been done if Christ were not the Being He eternally is. "Essential faith is belief in Christ. To deny either His person or His work is fatal."[1] Some of Christ's work is completed, some is now being done by Him, and some is to be done in the future.

All the work of Christ is the work of God. "The scheme of redemption began in the heart of God; the action in redemption is the action of God; it is God who sent Christ and God who is in Christ. The basis of everything is the love of God and the great desire of the heart of God that all men be saved (1 Timothy 2:4)."[2]

Had we been able to save ourselves, God would not have sent His Son to save us. Not once does this passage say that *we* have rescued ourselves, *we* have qualified ourselves to inherit with the saints, *we* have reconciled ourselves to God, or *we* can present ourselves holy. This passage is a thanksgiving to the Father who has done these things for us through Christ.

Who Christ Is and What He Has Done
Colossians 1:9-23

For this reason we also, since the day we heard it, do not cease to pray for you, and to ask that you may be filled with the knowledge of His will in all wisdom and spiritual understanding; that you may walk worthy of the Lord, fully pleasing Him, being fruitful in every good work and increasing in the knowledge of God; strengthened with all might, according to His glorious power, for all patience and longsuffering with joy; giving thanks to the Father who has qualified us to be partakers of the inheritance of the saints in the light. He has delivered us from the power of darkness and conveyed us into the kingdom of the Son of His love, in whom we have redemption through His blood, the forgiveness of sins. He is the image of the invisible God, the firstborn over all creation. For by Him all things were created that are in heaven and that are on earth, visible and invisible, whether thrones or dominions or principalities or powers. All things were created through Him and for Him. And He is before all things, and in Him all things consist. And He is the head of the body, the church, who is the beginning, the firstborn from the dead, that in all things He may have the preeminence.

For it pleased the Father that in Him all the fullness should dwell, and by Him to reconcile all things to Himself, by Him, whether things on earth or things in heaven, having made peace through the blood of His cross. And you, who once were alienated and enemies in your mind by wicked works, yet now He has reconciled in the body of His flesh through death, to present you holy, and blameless, and above reproach in His sight—if indeed you continue in the faith, grounded and steadfast, and are not moved away from the hope of the gospel which you heard, which was preached to every creature under heaven, of which I, Paul, became a minister.

As you read these verses again, remember that they were written to Christians. God's work has been done for all, but only those who receive the One through whom it was done can receive all the blessings that go with it.

The Work of God Through Jesus

Believers have been made qualified (competent) to be partakers of the inheritance of the saints in the light (1:12).
The inference here is that believers had not always been competent to inherit. It is God, through Christ, who has made us so. We are as unqualified to share in God's blessings as a paralyzed child in an iron lung is incapable of earning his food and shelter. But because of His only begotten Son, the Father includes us in His family and in His last will and testament.

Part of that inheritance is the hope stored up in heaven for us. Through faith in Christ, we are heirs of God in our present lives as well. The word *inheritance* refers to a part or portion that is given to those who are chosen to receive it. Just as the Psalmist wrote, "Jehovah is the portion of my inheritance and of my cup," Christians are given Christ Himself and can partake of Him daily (2 Peter 1:4). "The saints, possessed by Christ, themselves possess Christ as their riches and light, and are 'qualified' to do so by the grace of the Father who gave the Son for them and to them."[3] They can sing the modern "Psalm" by Fanny J. Crosby:

> Thou my everlasting portion,
> More than friend or life to me:
> All along my pilgrim journey,
> Savior let me walk with Thee.

Believers have been delivered from the power of darkness (1:13).
This fact is stated in past tense showing it has already happened. The word *delivered* may be translated "rescued," a description of being liberated from a life-threatening situation.

The phrase "power of darkness" refers to the tyrannical rule of Satan and his demons over the unsaved.[4] Some people think they are "their own person." But everyone, unless he has accepted Christ, is the captive of Satan. Through Adam, when he obeyed Satan rather than God, the principle of sin and death came into the world (Romans 5:12). Since then, every person except Jesus Christ has sinned. But through Christ, God has rescued believers from the power of Satan. God does not capture us against our wills, but will rescue us if we trust only Him to save us. We deceive ourselves if we *say* that we trust Him, but don't obey Him. One whose faith is only mental—not active—is in reality a spiritual corpse (James 2:26).

Satan continues to tempt Christians, but by trusting in the cross we can resist him, for it was by the cross that Christ stripped Satan of his power (2:15).

The devil makes many promises, but he is the father of liars (John 8:44). He can be compared to those who promised to fly citizens of a war-torn Central American country to the safety of the United States. The refugees paid for their transportation. Then the deceitful pilots left them in the desert to die a painful death. Like them, Satan extracts a high price from those he destroys. He promises escape from the disappointments and troubles of life, but he delivers death.

How does Satan accomplish this end? By tempting us with seemingly harmless and glamorous things. He appeals to our natural pride and entangles us in competitive struggles. Cunningly, he presents destructive seductions such as drugs, alcohol and illicit sex as escapes from the realities of life. But thanks to God's love, anyone can be saved from such a living death if he accepts the rescue offered in Christ.

Believers have been translated into the kingdom of Christ (1:13).

This is another of the changes that have already taken place for those who trust Christ. When a person accepts Christ, he is not a "man without a country." He doesn't have to pass naturalization tests. He immediately has citizenship under the rule of Christ. The word *translated* was used to describe the practice that sometimes occurred in the ancient world. That is, the monarch of one country would will his entire kingdom to the ruler of another country, and the transfer was immediate. But the transfer from

Satan's kingdom to Christ's kingdom is different in two respects: subjects of Satan have the choice as to which rule they will live under, and he doesn't turn them loose without a struggle. That is why this transfer God makes for believers is a rescue.

Believers have been given redemption, the forgiveness of their sins (1:14).

Notice the phrase "in whom" used here. It is only in union with Christ that redemption is possible. He died for the sins of the world, but acceptance of that death as a substitute for one's own death is on an individual basis. Only those who are "in Christ" are redeemed by Him. The word *redemption* refers to a transaction that produces freedom, but only at a cost. The return of an item that has been the security of a loan, such as might occur at a pawn shop when the loan is paid, is one form of redemption. In ancient times people who were taken as slaves because they could not pay their debts could be redeemed by payment of the debt. Always there was payment of a price before freedom could take place. The price of our freedom from sin was the life of Jesus Christ, and only in Him can we be liberated from sin (1 Peter 1:18-19).

The modifying phrase "the forgiveness of sins" explains the only process by which redemption is possible. Why do we need to have sins forgiven? If God were only as holy as the best person we know or have heard of, He would not necessarily have to forgive our sins in order to restore us to fellowship with Him. But He is absolutely holy and pure and demands sinlessness in His presence (Proverbs 15:9, 26). He does not overlook sin. Overlooking sin is only a counterfeit of forgiving sin. He forgives and forgets sins of those who accept Jesus Christ (Hebrews 10:17). He also forgives believers when we go astray from Him, then return and confess our sins. We don't have to attempt to straighten out our lives before returning to Him. If we confess our sin and sincerely determine to follow Him again, He will forgive us and provide the power to overcome sin, if we rely on Him.

All things have been created by Him (1:16).

The American Standard Version says that all things have been created both *in* and *through* Him. "The creation of all

39

things was *in* Him, as the effect was *in* the cause."[5] Not only was He the cause of creation, He was the agent of creation. He was in the beginning and was God then as well as now (John 1:1, 14). "In the beginning was the Word, and the Word was with God, and the Word was God. ... And the Word became flesh and dwelt among us." The first verse in the Bible says, "In the beginning God created the heavens and earth." The original word for *God* in that scripture and throughout the chapter is the plural form. As a person of the plural Godhead, Christ is creator. The entire first chapter of Genesis tells of the visible things He created.

Paul speaks of creation as being composed of two parts: things that are visible and things that are invisible. He lists some of the invisible things that have been created in Christ: thrones, powers, rulers and authorities. This list includes both heavenly and earthly systems of government. This means that Jesus is creator of angels and therefore far above them.

Not only did God establish the concept of obedience to authority in the visible and invisible realms, He gives the earthly kingdom to whomever He wishes and upholds the authority of nations (Daniel 4:17; Romans 13:1).

All things have been created for Christ (1:16).

The kingdoms of men will one day become the possession of Jesus Christ (Psalm 72:8-11; Revelation 11:15). Jesus was appointed heir of all things (Hebrews 1:2). This includes all things in both the physical and spiritual realms mentioned in verse 16. God does not revoke His gifts (Romans 11:29). He *shall* answer the prayer His beloved Son taught (Matthew 6:10).

All things hold together in Christ (1:17).

Wherever there is compatibility or union in the physical or spiritual world, Christ is the bond that holds together. He is the "gravity" that attracts things and persons to each other and to Himself. It has been discovered that all material things are made of atoms, and that atoms are made of particles of energy invisible to the naked eye. Hebrews 11:3 stated these facts almost 2,000 years ago: "the universe was formed at God's command, so that what is seen is not made out of what is visible." Some atoms have been brought together to form earth, others to form plants, others to form animate life, and so on throughout creation. Matter itself, although unstable, is held together by Christ.

God, through Christ, did not create the universe and then leave it on its own. Instead, Christ is upholding all things by the Word of His power (Hebrews 1:3 NIV). Some scientists consider that the "natural laws" of the universe are absolute, eternal, and cannot be broken. "The Bible sets forth a doctrine of divine providence, or care, for creation. The universe operates not according to impersonal, absolute laws but in response to the personal will of Christ. 'Natural law' is, in reality, what man can observe of Christ's personal control of the universe."[6]

All harmony and accord is the result of the work of Jesus, the Prince of Peace. Whenever there is peace between nations or individuals, whether it be tenuous or strong, it is Christ who is preserving and nurturing it. Genuine unity can be achieved only by letting Him draw us together in our thinking, goals and actions.

All things have been reconciled to God through Christ, who made peace with God through the cross (1:20).

The word "reconciled" means to change, or make different. The reconciliation spoken of here is reconciliation *to* God, not *with* God. God does not change; the thing being reconciled changes. This verse refers to things, not persons. Because Christ shed His blood on the cross, peace with God was made, so God could bring all things back to Himself. Peace with God is the foundation of all other peace.

When God created the universe and populated it, it was a moral universe. In God's words it was all "very good." When Adam and Eve sinned, the whole universe was changed: the ground was cursed, thorns and thistles were caused to grow, excessive labor was required to grow food, and pain in childbirth increased.

God's plan for a moral universe will not be thwarted. Now that peace has been made with God, creation will one day be changed back (reconciled) and be as He created it. There will be peace in the animal world; the nations of the earth will look to Christ; and all the earth will be filled with the knowledge of God (Isaiah 11:6-10). The whole creation is now in agony like birth pangs but confidently expects to

41

be changed (Romans 8:19-20). Because God sent His Son to die for the world and make peace with Him, the Babe of Bethlehem was heralded as the One who would bring peace on earth. This peace was prophesied by Isaiah (Isaiah 9:6-7).

Former enemies of God have been reconciled to Him (1:21-22).

Paul here tells Christians what took place in them because of their faith in Christ's death. The word *reconciled* in this verse is a stronger one than that in verse 20. This word means "changed completely." Those who don't trust in the cross are aliens, or estranged from God. To be a stranger to God is to be an enemy of God because "the mind of the flesh is enmity against God." There is no neutral ground. A person either thinks like God or he doesn't think like God.

Aliens are enemies to God in their minds, and this rebellious thinking produces evil acts. A complete change from the inside out was needed, and God accomplished this change through the blood of His Son. "What could never be achieved by willpower, headpower, or manpower is achieved by cross-power."[7] Christ didn't die just to inspire us to try to be better. He died to change us.

Oil and water don't mix, but by adding a detergent we can make an emulsion of them. The holy God and the sinful human race are not compatible, but God added the third ingredient, the blood of the cross, so we could be changed and brought back in union with Him.

Believers can be presented to God holy without blemish or accusation (1:22).

This was the purpose of Christ's suffering in His body. Coming into the presence of the Almighty God is an awesome thought. But we have the promise of Jesus that if we hear His Word and believe God, we now have eternal life and won't be judged, because we have already passed out of death into life (John 5:24). We have passed out of *our* death by means of *His* death, and into *His* life. It is God Himself who continually justifies those who believe in Christ, so who could condemn them before Him (Romans 8:31-34)? Believers can stand before God to receive reward. Disbelievers will appear there to be condemned.

These promises of God are sure. Christ's reconciling work has been completed on the cross, and His blood given there continues to cleanse those who put their trust in Him. He is now praying for the saints. He will come again and receive His own. This is Christ's work.

And what must mankind do to work the works of God? When asked this question, Jesus answered, "This is the work of God, that you believe in Him whom He sent" (John 6:28-29). Yes, that is all—believe, trust, and obey. When the Bible speaks of believing in Christ it means "to trust in, to rely upon, to cleave to" (Amplified Bible). If we truly do that, we will let Christ live His life in us. Following Christ may cause us to sacrifice as He sacrificed, to wait for God's timing as He waited, to get joy from doing only God's will as He did.

If we truly trust Him, we will overcome as He overcame. The one condition God sets is that believers continue to have faith in the cross of Christ. What an insult it would be to Jesus if we trusted the cross for a while, then stopped trusting it and depended on our own weak abilities or those of some other human being! One translation of verse 23 reads, "You must, of course, continue faithful on a firm and sure foundation, not allowing yourselves to be shaken from the hope you gained when you heard the Gospel."

Questions

1. Which sins does God overlook? Which sins will He forgive?
2. To whom are some of our sins a secret—to our fellowmen? to God? to us?
3. To what does the term *all things* in 1:16-17, 20 refer?
4. Who creates and maintains true unity in marriage, at work, in the church, and in creation? How do we avail ourselves of this unity?
5. What are your greatest needs?
6. By which specific power can Christ supply each need of ours?

Chapter 5

Colossians 1:24-2:3

Paul has told the Christians in Colosse about the love of God expressed in the life and death of His only begotten Son. If put in our words, the preceding paragraph says, "The universe, life, and all its blessings originated in this unique One, and in Him reside all perfect qualities. He has given all that He is and all that He has for our good and for all creation." Shouldn't these truths be enough to inspire believers to continue their life of faith? Yet, by inspiration of the Holy Spirit, Paul tells the Colossian church many times of his own personal love for them. The fact that God was working didn't relieve Paul of work. Rather, God's mighty work in Paul encouraged and enabled him to strive for the Colossians (1:29; 2:1). Paul's influence was much stronger because he allowed the love of God to flow through him. Ours will be stronger too, if we act in love as well as preach love.

God in His wisdom has provided the church, His body, to be an ideal environment for practicing love. He designed it so that, by looking to Jesus, it can solve its own problems and members can supply each other's needs (1 Corinthians 12:21). Much of the rest of the letter tells about relationships in the church: Paul's with the Colossians; Christ's with all His church; members with each other.

Throughout the letter Paul tells the church in Colosse how he practices love for them:

1:3, 9	He gives thanks and prays for them.
1:24	He suffers for them.
1:29; 2:1	He strives for them.
2:5	He is with them in spirit.

4:3	He seeks their prayers on his behalf.
4:7-17	He gives individual attention to some of them.
4:18	He signs the letter personally and asks for grace for them.

The scripture noted at the beginning of this chapter contains several themes. Four main ones are:

Paul's service to the church
God's mystery revealed
Acquiring knowledge and wisdom
Encouragement to faith

We will study the first two themes in this chapter and the last two in the next chapter.

Paul's Service to the Church
Colossians 1:24-25

> I now rejoice in my sufferings for you, and fill up in my flesh what is lacking in the afflictions of Christ, for the sake of His body, which is the church, of which I became a minister according to the stewardship from God which was given to me for you, to fulfill the word of God.

Paul was made a servant of the church by God Himself. He was commissioned by God to do a specific task, much like a manager or supervisor assigns certain duties to others. Paul was a prisoner at the time, yet he rejoiced because he was suffering for the sake of the church. Christians can have a deep, stable joy regardless of their circumstances. The awareness of the constancy of God's presence undergirds those who trust Him.

This consciousness is more valuable than any temporary amusement. Normal people want to be happy but often confuse the fun of pastimes with happiness. Trials are seen only as cause for unhappiness. But for those who trust God, trials are a means of obtaining true joy. That is because trials work *for* those who trust Christ rather than against them (2 Corinthians 4:16-18).

Having the right view of life in the light of eternity brings joy in the midst of pain or sorrow. Christians are not to think it strange when they have trouble. If they suffer *for Christ* they are to rejoice because they will have "exceeding joy" when Christ returns (1 Peter 4:12-14). Christ was afflicted and persecuted during His life on earth; why shouldn't His followers expect to suffer?

The word *sufferings* in chapter 1 verse 24 is never used in the Bible to refer to the sufferings of Christ on the cross. There is nothing lacking in His work of redemption. It is complete. At the time of His death, Jesus said, "It is finished."

The sufferings mentioned here are "the afflictions of Christ" which Paul experienced because of his union with Christ. The church is the emissary of Christ, so if Christ is wronged, its members suffer. If any member suffers, Christ suffers. When Paul was on the way to Damascus to persecute Christians there, Jesus appeared to him and did not ask, "Why are you persecuting the church?" but, "Why are you persecuting *Me*?" (Acts 9:1-5).

The specific ministry God gave Paul was to deliver His Word in full (1:25). The message he was to deliver at this time concerns the mystery which God revealed to him and to us through him.

God's Mystery Revealed
Colossians 1:25-2:3

I became a minister according to the stewardship from God which was given to me for you, to fulfill the word of God, the mystery which has been hidden from ages and from generations, but now has been revealed to His saints. To them God willed to make known what are the riches of the glory of this mystery among the Gentiles: which is Christ in you, the hope of glory. Him we preach, warning every man and teaching every man in all wisdom, that we may present every man perfect in Christ Jesus. To this end I also labor, striving according to His working which works in me mightily.

47

> For I want you to know what a great
> conflict I have for you and those in Laodi-
> cea, and for as many as have not seen my
> face in the flesh, that their hearts may be
> encouraged, being knit together in love,
> and attaining to all riches of the full
> assurance of understanding, to the
> knowledge of the mystery of God, both of
> the Father and of Christ, in whom are
> hidden all the treasures of wisdom and
> knowledge.

When the Bible speaks of a "mystery," it refers to something which has been unknown, then later revealed by God.
It does not refer to something forever hidden. The truths of
God are not made known to some secret order, or only to
the super-intelligent, or through some occult power. They
are revealed through God's servants, and many are recorded in the Bible for the benefit of *all* saints (1:26). Verse
28 states that Paul proclaimed this mystery "admonishing
and teaching *everyone* in *all* wisdom, so that we may present
everyone perfect in Christ" (NIV).

The mystery spoken of in these verses is a rich and
glorious one, and God is pleased to make it known (1:27).
This mystery is not a religious system, a theory, or a philosophy. It is a Person, and this Person can be *in* those who
trust Him. The mystery is "Christ in you"—the illustrious
One is actually in believers!

The result of having Christ within is the hope of glory
(1:27). This glory is the present possibility for Christians to
be transformed gradually during their lifetime by the reflection of Christ's glory (2 Corinthians 3:18). We will never
achieve perfection during this life, but this verse also refers
to the complete conformation to Him when He returns (Philippians 3:21; 1 John 3:2). Neither glory is possible without
"Christ in you." Christ within gives Christians not just a
desire for glory, but a "sure and steadfast hope" for glory.

One may ask, "Why do people need Christ *in* them to
have this hope when we have already been told that believers are in Christ? Isn't that sufficient?" One might also ask,
"How can a person receive Christ within?" To answer these
questions it is necessary to understand what God wants us

to be and the provision He has made for us to be that kind of people.

When God created mankind, it was in God's own image and likeness (Genesis 1:27). God's image and likeness is what He wants us to be. In the beginning, to accomplish this He personally breathed into Adam the breath of life (Genesis 2:7). This was not done in the case of animals (Genesis 1:24).

The word for "breath" means "vital spirit."[1] God's own Spirit vitalized the human race. As we learned in chapter 4, Christ was God in the beginning. "In the beginning was the Word, and the Word was with God, and the Word was God. He was in the beginning with God. All things were made through Him, and without Him nothing was made that was made" (John 1:1-3). Therefore, Jesus also gave life to Adam. One way in which humans are made in God's image is that we are threefold creatures, just as God is a threefold Being. The Godhead includes the Father, the Son and the Holy Spirit. We are composed of body, soul, and spirit (1 Thessalonians 5:23).

When Adam and Eve sinned, spiritual death came upon all mankind, sin entered the world, and physical death was appointed to all (Genesis 2:17; 3:6; Romans 5:12; Hebrews 9:27). Since then every person except Jesus Christ has sinned and is spiritually dead (Ephesians 2:1). A dead spirit allows sin to influence one's soul where mind and emotions reside and decisions are made. These decisions determine the behavior of one's body. Without Christ, spiritually, we are walking corpses no matter how active and well-behaved we may appear to be.

A person who is spiritually dead may be trained, much like an animal can be conditioned with rewards and punishments. "If all that we consist of is body and soul, then man is nothing more than a clever animal, and the natural man, in his 'unregenerate' condition, behaves as if this were so."[2] But humans are not animals (1 Corinthians 15:39). "It is your capacity to receive God, and to enjoy God and to be enjoyed by God which makes you man as opposed to mere animal, and it is only God in you that enables you to function as He intended you as man to function."[3]

Real life doesn't come from meditating upon one's own inner strength. It can't come from just attempting to do good any more than a person can give birth to himself or herself. Real life comes only from Christ within (1 John 5:11-12). Receiving the Spirit of God is one's spiritual resurrection. What we need is not just to be improved, but to be "*new* and improved." "We are not expected to change ourselves; it is the power of Christ which alone can change us."[4]

Modern psychology has discovered the truth that we need inner strength to achieve a feeling of fulfillment and satisfaction in life. Yet it rarely teaches Who is the Source of that strength. When people who are *dead* look inside themselves for strength for *life*, they can only find disappointment. If we are ever to attain fulfillment, we need not only *a* higher power within, but *the* highest power—Jesus Christ Himself. As in the beginning, it is still the vital Spirit of God within which brings us from death to life. It takes God to make a complete human being.

Spiritual life is dependent upon being in Christ and having Christ within, just as physical life depends upon being in air and having air in the lungs. Christianity is not an "outside-in" education and training of a person. It is an "inside-out" life: Christ's life within influences the whole person, spirit, soul and body.

To the question, "How can one receive Christ within?" we must answer that He is not indiscriminately given to all. It is not possible to *earn* this life. It cannot be absorbed by owning or wearing religious talismans or by meditating on self while sitting under a pyramid. Mere mental acquiescence that there is a "higher power" doesn't bestow this blessing. Such mental assent ignores Jesus Christ, who He is, and what He has done. One can receive Christ within only by believing what God says and putting complete, obedient trust in His Son (Ephesians 3:16-17).

In a future chapter we will learn how God works in the "burial" of the old "dead" person when that person trusts in Jesus Christ's death. We will also learn how God gives us new life.

Questions

1. Which members of Christ's body receive blessings? Which members should give blessings?
2. How can we discover God's mysteries today (1:26-29; Acts 17:11)?
3. Why do we need Christ's life within (Ephesians 2:1-6)?
4. Why do we sometimes ignore His life within us?

Chapter 6

Colossians 1:27-2:7

As we learned in chapter 5, the above passage contains four main themes. The first two were discussed in that chapter and the last two will be studied in this chapter. The four themes are:

Paul's service to the church
God's mystery revealed
Acquiring knowledge and wisdom
Encouragement to faith

Acquiring Knowledge and Wisdom
Colossians 1:27-2:3

To them God willed to make known what are the riches of the glory of this mystery among the Gentiles: which is Christ in you, the hope of glory. Him we preach, warning every man and teaching every man in all wisdom, that we may present every man perfect in Christ Jesus. To this end I also labor, striving according to His working which works in me mightily.

For I want you to know what a great conflict I have for you and those in Laodicea, and for as many as have not seen my face in the flesh, that their hearts may be encouraged, being knit together in love, and attaining to all riches of the full assurance of understanding, to the knowledge of the mystery of God, both of the Father and of

Christ, in whom are hidden all the treasures of wisdom and knowledge.

Again Paul emphasizes that his message from God is not a system of rules and rituals, but a Person—Jesus Christ. His ambition is for us to be perfect (1:28). The word translated "perfect" means "complete" or "mature." Changing us from being enemies of God to being reconciled to Him is not our work, but God's. Completing us and bringing us to maturity is also His work. Our part is to rely wholly upon Him. If we do that we will cooperate with Him.

It does not please God when we remain "babes in Christ" all our lives. Paul writes that he is helping Christians attain maturity by counseling and teaching them. The Greek word for warning means "to place in the mind" (translation by Bob Hendren). He wants us to receive into our minds the wisdom of Christ (1:28).

From verses 2 and 3 we may deduce that understanding Christ fully is possible when we have encouraged hearts and when we are united in love. Love is God's classroom. We are being trained in the schoolroom of love, and we have been united there.

The word translated "knit together" means "to be forced by association" or "to be bound together." Believers have been united with Christ by His death and resurrection. They have been forced into association with each other because He placed them together in the church.

We can visualize Christ artistically, deftly and lovingly entwining a variety of threads to make a useful, comforting garment. In a knitted fabric each stitch is dependent upon all the stitches surrounding it, while at the same time being essential to those stitches. In the same way, each Christian performs a necessary function in the church, while being dependent upon all other members of the body. In knitting, whenever a stitch is "dropped" the tear in the cloth becomes larger unless it is mended. As head of the body, Christ is able to mend all torn or weakened areas.

As builder of His church, He is much like an experienced stone mason who can shape different kinds and sizes of rocks so that they fit together to construct a sturdy building. He does not mold us against our wills, but if we let Him, He will fit us in His church and bind us together with the mortar of His love.

It is in this union with Christ and each other that we learn our need for love. We discover that God is the Source of love, and we learn how to receive and express love. We understand forgiveness, patience and humility through that union. "No intellectual process will lead to an assured grasp of spiritual truth, unless it be accompanied by love. ... This unity of love will lead to full knowledge of the mystery of God."[1]

If we return God's love, He can teach us what He wants us to know about Jesus Christ. This loving relationship gives one a full and complete understanding of Christ (2:2). Thus it becomes possible for Christians to share their knowledge of Christ; together, they come to know Him deeply and therefore act wisely. A Christian who doesn't habitually associate with other Christians is denying himself or herself an opportunity to mature.

The Greek word for "wisdom" used in these verses is based on the word which means "clear." We can see, then, that wisdom dispels foggy thinking and gives us a clear view of things as they really are—things of the universe, things of the mind and things of the spirit. Without wisdom, our view of what goes on around us can be as distorted as those on television of persons whose identity must be hidden. If our knowledge is gained by only worldly experience, we are like children not yet tall enough to see the parade pass by.

One cannot reach maturity without knowing Christ because in Him "are hidden all the treasures of wisdom and knowledge" (2:3). Nowhere else is there wisdom worth seeking. Since the beginning, the only light mankind can have is Christ's life (John 1:4). Outside Him there is no real insight. When it comes to acquiring wisdom, no amount of meditation, education or orientation can compare to knowing Christ Himself.

Jesus said, "If you love me you will keep my commandments." Our beginning infantile love, when we first became Christians, prompted us to obey Him; with each act of obedience we know Him better, and thus love Him more. Therefore, our lives can become an increasingly strong circle of spiritual growth: love for Christ leads to obeying Him, which leads to knowing Him better, then to loving Him more, and again to obeying Him—repeated in an endless cycle.

Loving, grateful obedience brings about maturity if such obedience is uninterrupted by doubt. The importance of faithfully holding to Christ will be discussed in the next chapter.

Things that don't make sense to the natural mind may actually be very wise. Paul writes in another letter that the wisdom of this world is foolishness with God, and that the only way anyone can become wise in this world is to consider Himself to be a fool (1 Corinthians 3:18-19). Only then can he go to Jesus, the Source of wisdom, and be confident in *Him.* James writes that if we ask God for wisdom He will give it to us (James 1:5).

It is easy for our minds to confuse feelings of success or the accumulation of knowledge with genuine wisdom. Examples of this misunderstanding can be found in the business and education fields. Even the most knowledgeable financial moguls, publicized as expert, sometimes make headlines by becoming bankrupt. Experienced educators present long-thought-out plans to solve the problems of public schools. Many of these plans become just one more link in a long chain of failures.

Even in individual small ways, if we feel temporary satisfaction and pride, we can be deceived into believing the great lie which Satan sold in Eden and continues to market today. That lie is that man can be his own god because he can be as wise as God, and that sin is good (Genesis 3:4-5).

We can escape this ignorant lie and the destruction it brings if we sincerely love truth, if we trust ourselves to Him who is the Truth, and if we act on the truths God presents in the Bible (John 14:6; 2 Thessalonians 2:9-12).

Wisdom is not possible without accurate knowledge. However, it is possible to know *about* Christ without *knowing* Christ. "We have to do a great deal more than just believe truths about Christ. We must receive Christ if we are to have life. ... To believe on the Son of God involves such complete submission to Jesus Christ that all things are taken note of according to the mind and viewpoint of Christ."[2] Trench wrote, "The man of 'knowledge' may stop with mere sight of truth; the man of 'wisdom' reflects upon it, receives it, in a way affecting character and action."[3]

Chapter 2 verse 3 states that all treasures of wisdom and knowledge are hidden in Christ. This statement doesn't mean that these treasures cannot be found, but that Christ is the storehouse of wisdom and knowledge. We can never exhaust the supply. "Oh, the depth of the riches both of the wisdom and the knowledge of God! How unsearchable are His judgments" (Romans 11:33).

Not to avail ourselves of these inexhaustible treasures would be like starving while standing in the midst of a well-stocked pantry. If anyone wants to learn to live wisely, he must go deeper into the heart and mind of Jesus. Only by knowing Him intimately can one learn to cope with every kind of trouble; to enjoy every blessing and trial; to get along with strangers, neighbors and family. Only Christ's wisdom can equip us to make the right decisions on political, social and moral issues. Receiving these treasures depends upon our faith.

Encouragement to Faith
Colossians 2:4-7

Now this I say lest anyone should deceive you with persuasive words. For though I am absent in the flesh, yet I am with you in spirit, rejoicing to see your good order and the steadfastness of your faith in Christ.

As you therefore have received Christ Jesus the Lord, so walk in Him, rooted and built up in Him and established in the faith, as you have been taught, abounding in it with thanksgiving.

Paul warns about those who want to deceive Christians with grandiose arguments. He writes that his own spirit makes him feel as if he were with the Colossians, and that he can see their (army-like) "good order" of spiritual defenses and their steadfast faith in Christ. Such faith will protect against the false teaching he warns against in the next part of the letter. It is in faith that one receives Christ, and it is in faith that one must conduct his life (2:6).

There are three words used in verse 7 to describe Christians' union with Christ. Christians have been "rooted" in Him, thus permitting them to continually partake of His life. They are being "built up" in Him. God is the master builder, and He is working toward their completion. They are "established" (strengthened) in faith, as well. Their foundation and completion is based in faith and therefore firm. The Colossians' faith was in what they had been taught, "the truth of the Gospel" (1:5).

Today we have the truth of the Gospel in the Bible from the beginning to end. All that is recorded before the cross points toward that great event. All that is recorded since the cross is based on the Gospel of the cross. Through prayerful study, we can grasp that cornerstone of the Bible and by faith make it the touchstone of our lives.

"Abounding in it with thanksgiving" is not just an added thought (2:7). Gratitude is the fuel that energizes one for living in Christ. Knowing about God doesn't necessarily produce a life that glorifies God, unless gratitude accompanies that knowledge. A thankless heart can result in useless, empty thinking, which in turn prevents us from seeing what really makes sense (Romans 1:21).

On the other hand, each time we feel and express gratitude to Him is an acknowledgment of the reality that God's ways are high above our ways. By sincere thanksgiving we reinforce our belief that God is love.

A review of the passage studied in the last two chapters, listing the positive words and phrases, will impress upon our minds the many things believers have in Christ for which to be thankful, such as joy, hope, and fullness. How different these blessings are from the effect of false doctrines, all of which are fathered by Satan. False doctrines cause futility, fear and anxiety. Christians have been rescued from Satan, and God has given them everything they need for life.

> His divine power has given to us all things that pertain to life and godliness, through the knowledge of Him who called us by glory and virtue, by which have been given to us exceedingly great and precious promises, that through these you may be partakers of the divine nature, having escaped the corruption that is in the world through lust.
>
> 2 Peter 1:3-4

Questions

1. Can one become wise without having faith in Jesus Christ?
2. What part does faith play in obedience (Hebrews 11:6)?
3. What part does obedience play in problem solving?
4. What part does obedience play in knowing God?
5. What part does knowing God play in loving Him?
6. What part does loving God play in obedience?
7. Can one become mature without active faith in Jesus Christ?

Chapter 7

Colossians 2:8-15

This chapter and the one following discuss the above scriptures. You should read all of these verses before continuing your study. There are four main themes covered by this passage:

1. The changes that have been made in and for believers
2. How one can be in Christ and have Christ within
3. Warnings about false teachers
4. The nature of the body of Christ

This chapter will comment on the first two points and the next chapter will discuss the last two. Verse 8 will be studied with the warnings given in verses 16-23. Therefore, this lesson is mainly from verses 9-15.

Six changes that have been made in and for Christians are mentioned in verses 9-15:

Christians have been given completeness in Christ.
Christ "circumcised" them.
God unites them with Christ's resurrection.
God forgives their sins.
The cross canceled the guilt of the law.
Christ disarmed Satan's kingdom.

Colossians 2:8-13

Beware lest anyone cheat you through philosophy and empty deceit, according to the traditions of men, according to the basic principles of the world, and not according to Christ. For in Him dwells all the fullness of the Godhead bodily; and you are complete in Him, who is the head of all principality and power.

In Him you were also circumcised with the circumcision made without hands, by putting off the body of the sins of the flesh, by the circumcision of Christ, buried with Him in baptism, in which you also were raised with Him through faith in the working of God, who raised Him from the dead. And you, being dead in your trespasses and the uncircumcision of your flesh, He has made alive together with Him, having forgiven you all trespasses.

Christians Are Given Fullness in Christ

Verse 9 reads, "*in Him* dwells all the fullness of the Godhead bodily." Christ was not merely a recipient of some form of divinity because He received His physical life from God and shares that divinity with every kind of life, the source of which is God. This verse means that the complete Deity resides continuously in Christ. "The Greek word translated 'Godhead' (or Deity) occurs nowhere else in the New Testament. This word refers not to an attribute, but to the essential fact of Deity. ... It is not enough to say that Christ was Divine ... There is a sense in which every man is 'Divine' but it cannot be said of every man that he is Deity. Deity is the essential, peculiar, lonely nature of God."[1]

The Godhead is three Persons in one: the Father, the Son and the Holy Spirit. Since the beginning, Jesus has been God the *Father.* "In the beginning was the Word, and the Word was with God, and the Word was God" (John 1:1). He came to earth and took physical form making Him man, the Son (Philippians 2:7-8). John the Baptist testified that Jesus was the *Son* of God because he saw the *Holy Spirit* descend and remain on Him (John 1:32-34). The word translated "dwells" in verse 9 can be translated "remains." All three Persons of the Deity are embodied in Christ. We cannot fully understand how one Being is three Persons. But this fact can be accepted by faith, perhaps the ultimate faith.

Faith believes what it doesn't understand. It is not our place to decide, after consideration, if God's Word is true, wise or fitting. Our place is to believe that it is all these things because it is God's, and to follow it. Then we will learn from experience that it is true, wise and fitting. Our faith must be in the mind of God, not in our "second guessing." Real faith obeys. It acts out of trust and devotion.

Whether or not we understand, we must believe that all the fullness of Deity dwells in Jesus bodily, or we cannot be made complete (2:10). We must also believe that we need to be made complete. "He is not made full, He is full. The saints are not full, they are made full. ... We are made full in Him; for it is in Christ that we are restored to our true place in creation; in Christ that we are restored to that fellowship with God that means cooperation with all His purpose."[2]

Why do we need to be restored and made full? Wouldn't it be sufficient to just add some Christian values to the lives of well-intentioned people? This would benefit society, but would not save a single person from perishing. We need to be made full because we are empty—completely empty.

Since Adam, every person except Jesus Christ has sinned in every aspect of his or her being—in body, in soul, and in spirit (Romans 3:23). "In describing the total sinfulness of mankind which doesn't put trust in God, Paul writes that we dishonor our *bodies*. Next he says our passions (*emotions*) are shameful. He adds that our *minds* are depraved (Romans 1:24-28)."[3]

Emotions, mind and will function within our *souls* which are interwoven with our *spirits*. "As mankind is abandoned in his *physical* sin and his *emotional* sin, so he is also abandoned to his *intellectual* sin. ... In other words, we have sinned as total beings."[4] The Deity filled Jesus, and our threefold natures—spirit, soul and body—need to receive the fullness only Christ can give us.

Paul's description in Romans 1:24-28 and 3:23 of the depravity of mankind doesn't alter the fact that as humans made in God's image we have innate worth. The cross of Christ and God's gift of the Holy Spirit to live within us are proof of that. God thinks we are worth being made holy.

God is not a seamstress who alters His truth so that it will fit us. Neither is He a mechanic who attempts to install Cadillac parts into our Model-T existence. If we allow Him to do so, He can change every aspect of our sinful beings. This transformation first takes place in our hearts.

God's method of saving us is to reach our hearts through our bodies. We must first hear who Christ is before we can trust Him. Belief comes by hearing the Word of God (Romans 10:17). Sometimes we are attracted to Christ by seeing Him portrayed in the life of a Christian. Our *physical* ears and eyes are involved. Hearing from the Bible what Christ has done allows the Holy Spirit to convince us we have wronged God and can cause us to feel sorrow toward Him. If our *emotions* are affected in this way, we will want to admit our sinfulness (2 Corinthians 7:10-11; Acts 2:37-38). This change of *mind*—this sincere decision of allegiance to God—permits Him to do what He wants to do—that is, to save us and to make our *spirits* alive.

Alas, Satan uses this same method to destroy us. Through Eve's ears and eyes he presented to her the false "benefits" of disobedience to God. She listened, then looked at the forbidden fruit. It appealed to her fleshly desires— *physical* hunger, love of *appearance* and *mental* ambition. She obeyed self and Satan rather than God and was fully controlled by sin (Genesis 3:1-6).

The devil tempts us in the same ways today. The question is: shall we listen to and be moved by Satan, the spirit of disobedience, or by the message of Christ and His Spirit (Ephesians 2:2-3)?

After becoming Christians, we are still tempted to rebel against God. If we don't set our minds to desire what the Holy Spirit desires for us, we will not be complete. If we willfully resist Him, we won't have the full, mature life that can be ours (Romans 8:5).

How One Can Be In Christ and Have Christ Within

Just as the Godhead filled Jesus, our threefold nature— spirit, soul and body—can receive the fullness of Christ. This filling is made possible by faith in the work of God (2:12). The specific work we must have faith in is God's resurrecting Jesus. Of course, His resurrection necessitated His death and burial beforehand.

Those who have faith in Christ's resurrection do not have to experience deserved execution because of their sins. Instead, they can be buried into *His* death. God placed our sins on Him. Therefore, He had to die (Isaiah 53:6).

If we accept His death as being in place of ours, we must be buried into His death (Romans 6:3-4). Burial of Christ's body was proof of His death. In the same way, burial by baptism of one who has faith in Christ's death is the outward evidence of that faith.

The word *baptize* means "to cover wholly with fluid."[5] How foolish we would be to say we trust Christ as our personal Lord, then neglect doing the first thing He asks of us—being baptized. On the other hand, it is impossible to be truly baptized without having faith in His death and resurrection, no matter how deeply we may be buried in water.

Romans 6:3 and Galatians 3:27 state that believers are baptized into Christ, and into Christ's death. Because of the cross, baptism—this one act of faith—puts a believer into Christ and puts Christ into him or her. In addition, God adds to the church those who have this saving faith (Acts 2:47).

What a wonderful, merciful exchange God has made. By placing our sins on the sinless Jesus Christ, making Him to be sin on our behalf, He has made it possible for us to become the righteousness of God in Him (2 Corinthians 5:21). But God doesn't force His righteousness on anyone, and no one receives it without the conviction that he needs it as well as Christ's substitutionary death.

Christ "Circumcises" Christians

Jesus can liberate us from our fleshly human nature if we put our faith in His death. Just as physical circumcision done by human hands removes flesh, the circumcision done by Christ removes our inherently fleshly nature (2:11). True circumcision is that of the heart (Romans 2:29).

Fleshly nature is opposed to God's Spirit and behaves in unloving, malicious and destructive ways (Galatians 5:19-21). Christ reconciled sinners to God in His sinless body (1:22), and the body of the believer's fleshly nature must be killed and disposed of. Only Christ can do this, but we must submit to Him. "Submit to death, death of your ambitions and favorite wishes every day and death of your whole body in the end; submit with every fiber of your being and you will find eternal life. ... Nothing in you that has not died will ever be raised from the dead."[6]

God Unites Christians to Christ's Resurrection

Baptism is not only a burial but is also a resurrection of a new person in Christ as surely as Christ was raised by God from the dead. The grave is the place He took our sins, so it is fitting that our whole being be buried with Him. Then we can be made alive with Him (Romans 6:4). Colossians 2:12 and 13 state that believers were buried *with* Him, raised *with* Him and made alive *with* Him.

Inward faith displayed in outward baptism makes believers one with Christ and God. Believers are promised that if they have a change of mind (repent) and are baptized, they will receive the Holy Spirit, Himself, as a gift (Acts 2:38). It is only through baptism that we receive Christ within, for it is then that His Spirit is given to us. If we don't limit Him, His Spirit within can fill our whole being. This is our hope of glory (1:27). It is His Spirit that produces in us the attitudes and actions of eternal life (Galatians 5:22-23). His Spirit convicts, leads and enables all those who allow Him to do so.

How wonderful that God has united us with Christ in His death, burial and resurrection! How sad to remain united with Satan in death! There will be no resurrection from burial with Satan in death (Revelation 20:10, 14).

Colossians 2:13-15

And you, being dead in your trespasses and the uncircumcision of your flesh, He has made alive together with Him, having forgiven you all trespasses, having wiped out the handwriting of requirements that was against us, which was contrary to us. And He has taken it out of the way, having nailed it to the cross. Having disarmed principalities and powers, He made a public spectacle of them, triumphing over them in it.

God Forgives Christians' Sins;
The Cross Canceled the Guilt of the Law

It is only because of faith in the death and resurrection of Jesus that Christians "have been unconditionally forgiven of all their trespasses," as the original language says (2:13). For those who rely on His death, it has erased the *charges* that were against them because they trespass the Ten Commandments and ordinances of the law. God's law is spiritual, but human nature is fleshly and sinful. Therefore its regulations are contrary to us (Romans 8:6-8).

Whenever we are disobedient we feel guilt. It is instinctive with human beings that we try to place that guilt on someone or something else. We say that circumstances, some person, or even the devil "made me do it." Graciously, God has provided the only place where our guilt can be completely taken away—the cross of Christ.

On the cross, Christ paid the penalty for our disobedience to God's law, making it possible for our guilt to be taken away. It no longer comes between God and those who trust in the saving power of the cross. This permits their union with God (2:14).

Christ Disarmed Satan's Kingdom

By the cross, Christ proved He is the head of all principalities and powers. He stripped those authorities of their strength (2:15). These authorities and powers are the supernatural rulers of the "kingdom of darkness" spoken of in Ephesians 6:12 and Colossians 1:13. They include those in both human and supernatural realms whose authority comes from Satan. It was through Christ's death that He annulled the power of the devil, the one who had the power of death (Hebrews 2:14). He exposed (made a public spectacle of) Satan by being seen many times after His resurrection, thus proving that death had been conquered (1 Corinthians 15:3-8).

The devil's sentence is that, after Christ returns, he will be cast into the lake of fire and brimstone which has been prepared for him (Revelation 20:10; Matthew 25:41). But at the present he "walks about like a roaring lion seeking whom he may devour" (1 Peter 5:8). If we depend on Christ's Spirit, He will save us because "He who is in you is greater than he who is in the world" (1 John 4:4).

God has limited the power of our enemy, Satan. If we have put our faith in Christ's death, He has erased the record of our sins. He has given us Christ's fullness. Therefore we, too, are as well-equipped as the best oceangoing vessel. If we continue to depend upon the guidance, power, and completeness of Jesus Christ and His Spirit within, we can navigate safely and joyfully through life to the destination He is preparing for us.

Questions

1. Does God save anyone who doesn't want to be saved (1 Timothy 2:4; Mark 1:14-15; Romans 10:10)?
2. What was proof of Christ's death (John 19:31-42)?
3. What was proof of Christ's resurrection (1 Corinthians 15:3-8)?
4. What is proof of our love for Christ (John 14:15)?

Chapter 8

Colossians 2:8-23

In chapter 7 we discovered that the above verses contain the following points:

1. The changes that have been made in and for believers
2. How one can be in Christ and have Christ within
3. Warnings about false teachers
4. The nature of the body of Christ

This chapter will discuss the last two points. Verses 2:8 and 16-23 show that the false teachers in Colosse believed themselves to be above others and claimed to have experiences others did not have. Some of them treated their bodies with severity in an attempt to become pure (2:20-22). Others, knowing that through their own efforts it is impossible to become pure enough to be accepted by God, behaved with complete license and practiced no restraints. Both the licentious and the ascetic believed the lie that salvation can be earned.

Through Paul, God warned Christians that salvation has been made possible only by the cross of Christ; the union with Christ ensures salvation for those who believe in Him.

Warnings about False Teachers
Colossians 2:8-23

Beware lest anyone cheat you through philosophy and empty deceit, according to the tradition of men, according to the basic principles of the world, and not according to Christ. For in Him dwells all the fullness of the Godhead bodily; and you are complete in Him, who is the head of all principality and power.

In Him you were also circumcised with the circumcision made without hands, by putting off the body of the sins of the flesh, by the circumcision of Christ, buried with Him in baptism, in which you also were raised with Him through faith in the working of God, who raised Him from the dead. And you, being dead in your trespasses and the uncircumcision of your flesh, He has made alive together with Him, having forgiven you all trespasses, having wiped out the handwriting of requirements that was against us, which was contrary to us. And He has taken it out of the way, having nailed it to the cross. Having disarmed principalities and powers, He made a public spectacle of them, triumphing over them in it.

So let no one judge you in food or in drink, or regarding a festival or a new moon or sabbaths, which are a shadow of things to come, but the substance is of Christ. Let no one cheat you of your reward, taking delight in false humility and worship of angels, intruding into those things which he has not seen, vainly puffed up by his fleshly mind, and not holding fast to the Head, from whom all the body, nourished and knit together by joints and ligaments, grows with the increase that is from God.

Therefore, if you died with Christ from the basic principles of the world, why, as though living in the world, do you subject yourselves to regulations—"Do not touch, do not taste, do not handle," which all concern things which perish with the using according to the commandments and doctrines of men? These things indeed have an

appearance of wisdom in self-imposed religion, false humility, and neglect of the body,
but are of no value against the indulgence
of the flesh.

Since God loves us, He doesn't leave us on our own
once we have become Christians; He protects us and warns
us of specific dangers. In verse 8, He tells the Christians at
Colosse to be alert to anyone who teaches ideas that are
based on worldly principles.

The Prince of the world is Satan, and he has nothing in
Christ (John 14:30). He and his followers can capture
Christians or "make spoil" of them, as some versions read,
much like a conquering army can weaken and disable an
enemy, then make off with the valuables, or spoils, of the
conquered country.

No matter how much Satan's teachers may sound as if
they are representatives of God, they are not, because their
philosophy is not based on Christ. They may vaguely, or
even devotedly, refer to God while denying who the Son of
God is. Such philosophy is useless, non-productive, and
empty. Placed against a life under Satan, the fullness we
can have in Christ is like a tropical rain forest as compared
to an arid desert.

Doctrine of false teachers originates with humans, not
God. Therefore, it is deceitful and has no lasting value. It
is pure humanism, always a threat to the minds of people.
Fallen mankind is easy prey to humanism in its many
forms.

When the Christian becomes steeped
in the futile wisdom of the world, vainly
puffed up in his fleshly mind, he will seek
refuge in the world's rudiments, in pagan
philosophy, in poets' sentiments, in art in
music, in logic and disputations of
self-conceit. He will begin to talk about
"psychology" and "character-building" and
"self-culture" and "will-power" and "forma-
tion of habits," and about politics and so-
ciology. ... These things never did save, and
never will, until man can lift himself up by

his own bootstraps. And they hope to com-
pass the salvations of men's souls by that
message of death! ... Where is the trans-
forming power of "Christ in you, the hope
of glory" and the teaching concerning the
"Spirit of life in Christ Jesus"? And when
the gospel is taught, it is with such an
affectation of great deepness and in such
adulteration with human philosophy that
the cross of Christ is made of none effect (1
Corinthians 1:17).[1]

May we yield to the conviction that the Holy Spirit tries
to impress upon our hearts. Only then will we stop defend-
ing human arrogance. Mankind in submission to God is
God's greatest creation. When we rebel against Him, we
become incorrigible degenerates.

The word *therefore* in verse 16 refers to the preceding
paragraph. Since Christ has stripped Satan of his power,
and since Christians have been united with Christ, they
should let no one judge or "umpire" them, as the original
language means, by man-made rules. Abstaining from certain meats and drinks and observing special days were
ordained by God under the Mosaic law. Now that the real
thing—Jesus Christ—has come, there is no need for the
rituals that pointed toward His coming. The false teachers
at Colosse had not begun to worship God "in spirit and in
truth." Like children arguing about the rules of the game
instead of playing it, they were trying to force the Colossian
Christians to worship through humanly devised procedures.

Abstention as a religious rite may create an appearance
of wisdom and holiness. But this so-called "humility" and
self-imposed worship only makes one aware of himself and
of what *he* is doing. When people worship in this way they
cannot be thinking of God, but only of self.

The word translated "self-imposed religion" is defined as
being "voluntarily adopted worship, not that which is im-
posed upon others, but which one affects."[2] Forced worship
is hollow worship. When a person truly knows God and
Christ, his or her being is filled to overflowing with devotion
to God.

Christians should not let anyone rob them of what is rightfully theirs through their faith in the cross. These possessions include eternal life, received when they accepted the Son, and the hope for a rich welcome into His eternal kingdom (2 Peter 1:10-11). These blessings could be stolen if one only pretends to be humble, or if one worships angels.

One duty of angels is to serve Christians, not to be objects of their worship. Hebrews 1:14 reads, "Are they (angels) not all ministering spirits sent forth to minister for those who will inherit salvation?" God's angels act on His order and will do nothing contrary to His Word. According to Jesus, angels protect childlike believers and are in constant contact with God on behalf of their safety (Matthew 18:10).

The function of angels has been known to include waking and feeding a prophet (1 Kings 19:7), giving therapy to Jesus (Matthew 4:1-11), delivering messages, and many more services. We are grateful for the myriad of God's angels, but we are not to worship them—not even the one who will announce the marriage supper of the Lamb (Revelation 18:21; 19:9-10).

Verse 18 warns against anyone who tells in great detail about visions they claim to have seen. "The phrase 'intruding into those things which he has not seen,' means that the false teacher 'invades the region of the unseen with a presumptuous assertion as if he *had* seen it.' ... The Apostle (Paul) denies such a claim."[3] Many scholars translate that phrase, "dwelling on things he has seen." The original word for "has seen" is *stared at.* For false teachers, visions became the center of their attention and the foundation of their faith. Full of self-importance, they became inflated with pride. Their minds were centered on these "visions," and to them, Christ was not the Head (2:19). Therefore they could not know truth, for all the treasures of wisdom and knowledge are in Him (2:3).

Today, many religions emphasize formalities and promote their programs. Their own experiences are most important, and their rituals become an end in themselves. In some religions, transcendental meditation, the eating of health foods for religious purposes and the practice of yoga are worshiped.

Even within Christianity, we see those who claim to possess special powers or know revelations in addition to the Bible. Some say they have received confidential prophecies delivered by messengers of God. Others profess to have the power of healing within themselves. These people are worshiped by some.

The church, good deeds, baptism and assembly sometimes receive the homage that should be given to Christ Himself. It is easy for us to think that what we are doing, ostensibly for Christ, is more important than Christ Himself.

The story of Mary and Martha in Luke 10 illustrates how dedicated Christians get "off-center." Martha was distracted, or "dragged around" as the Greek word states, by the frustrations of serving Jesus (translation by Bob Hendren). Mary chose the better way, which was to know Jesus better by being with Him and learning from His words. Jesus approved of Mary's behavior and chided Martha for her anxiety.

Those who have died with Christ to the fundamental principles of this age have no reason to subject themselves to the outward show of wisdom, such as not handling, tasting, or touching so-called "evil" things (2:20-21). Such outward practices will not protect one from falling when attacked by Satan or by his own fleshly nature. Only complete trust in Christ within can guard from this ever-present danger.

The Nature of the Body of Christ

The body of Christ must hold fast to its Head. Cleaving to Christ makes it possible to grow with the right kind of growth (Ephesians 5:23). Each person who has been joined to Christ has direct and immediate access to Him, just as each member of a healthy human body has direct and immediate access to its brain. No member has priority over another in contacting the Head. Christ has made a healthy church; ideally, it operates just as a healthy human body operates through its bones, ligaments and nerves (2:19).

"When the children of God are filled with the fullness of God they will find themselves harmonizing with one another. ... When Christ is truly made the Head of the church, when His presence and authority are recognized, everything

74

is different."[4] A member who is holding fast to the Head continually communicates with the Head and is protected from false doctrine.

One who does not hold fast to Christ can become sick, immobile and without feeling, just as a part of a human body does when communication with its brain is interrupted. A whole congregation may grow in numbers and reputation by operating on worldly principles, but it will be a malignant growth rather than the kind of growth God supplies, if it doesn't hold fast to Christ. This abnormal growth may be interesting for a while, or even attractive, like the scarring of a tree which an artist might portray on canvas. But if not healed, the scar will cause the death of the tree.

Sincere Christians will ask, "How can we recognize a false religion?" From these verses we learn that false religions can be recognized by at least two things: they do not give Jesus Christ the place God has given Him, or they claim to have revelations above and beyond the Bible. They do this by teaching that Christ is not all-sufficient for human needs. They say that something in addition to Christ is needed, or that Christ is not needed at all. A person who claims to have visions or to receive revelations contrary to the Bible is putting himself above others, above even the apostles and prophets.

God gave Christ the place of supremacy; God called Him His Son. A religion that does not confess Jesus as God's Son, the Christ, is certainly from Satan (1 John 4:1-6). A religion that de-emphasizes the cross of Christ is an affront to God because the cross cost Him so dearly.

A message that is not Christ-centered and a life that is not Christ-centered are as out of harmony with God and His Word as a phonograph record with its hole off-center. The person who has died with Christ and has been raised with Him needs only to hold to Christ. Then, although he will be in discord with the world, he will make melody with God and with others in God's church.

Questions

1. Why are Christians sometimes tempted to thoughtlessly follow those who proclaim themselves to be intelligent, wise or mature (2 Timothy 4:3; John 3:19-21)?

75

2. How are Christians enabled to resist temptations (Philippians 2:12-13; Acts 2:38; Galatians 5:25; Hebrews 7:25)?
3. What three practices can help Christians hold to Christ (Philippians 4:6; Psalm 119:11; Romans 12:10)?
4. Under God's arrangement, which members of the body of Christ are to control the thinking and actions of other members (Philippians 2:1-8; 1 Peter 1-3)?
5. Define humanitarianism. Describe its many forms.

Chapter 9

Colossians 3:1-11

Christians are different from other people and even from the people they themselves once were. They are now different because they are united with Christ, possess His life within and have hope for the future (1:5).

There is a story about a young man named Charlie who inherited the large farm which had been owned by his family for many generations. Looking to the future, he married.

Charlie maintained the buildings and fences of his farm and used his skills to cultivate abundant crops. For several years he was the most prosperous farmer in the community. His only disappointment was that he and his wife had no children.

Soon Charlie's neighbors noticed that his buildings needed repair, his herds were diminished and his crops failed. It finally became necessary to sell a parcel of his land each year to pay taxes.

Charlie and his wife still had no children, and he became despondent and saw no reason to go on. He was called a failure as a farmer. Then his wife died.

Some time later, a young woman came to the community to visit a relative of hers. Charlie was attracted to her, and they were married. A year later, a great change took place in Charlie. He was seen painting his house, spraying the orchard and buying more cattle.

A friend said to him, "Charlie, we're glad you are feeling better. Do you mind telling us what made the difference?"

"I'm glad to," Charlie answered. "In five months there will be a little Charlie at our house. Then will come my grandson, Charles III, then Charles IV, and so on. My life will go on. Knowing that makes a man want to try his best."

Our hope as Christians is more sure and lasting than Charlie's hope in yet unborn descendants. Because we have Christ's life, we can do more than just "try our best"—we can submit to that Power within us.

When we were baptized into Christ's death, God didn't anesthetize us and implant Christ's life into our being. We consciously submitted our wills to God's will. At that time, we believed that we needed to be saved and that God had placed our sins on Jesus. At that same time, we believed that Jesus died in our place, was raised, and that God, through the Holy Spirit within, gave us all that Christ is, thereby giving us hope for daily living and for eternity. God didn't give us the saving life of Jesus in piecemeal bits. This gracious gift was a "package deal" which we received by faith when we became Christians (2:11-13). It will be lost only if we lose faith and ignore Him or try to add, by our own efforts, to the all-sufficiency of Christ. Now that we are Christians, we can enjoy the completeness that we have in Christ (2:10), only if we continue to consciously submit our wills to Christ's will.

The third chapter of the book of Colossians tells us how to let go of the old life and let Christ live His life in us. He unconditionally forgives believers, so, out of gratitude, we should work toward the goals listed here. Striving toward such virtues demands prayer.

God has opened a highway of communication between Himself and Christians, yet we sometimes build barricades. If we keep a thankful, humble attitude, we can make no mistakes in our requests to Him. He listens, He hears, He acts. He will answer in the right way, at the right time.

Colossians 3:1-4

If then you were raised with Christ, seek those things which are above, where Christ is, sitting at the right hand of God. Set your minds on things above, not on things on the earth. For you died, and your life is hidden with Christ in God.

When Christ who is our life appears, then
you also will appear with Him in glory.

Since Christians have been made new by being united
with Christ in His resurrection, the starting point for the
future is having the right mind-set. Earthly, temporary things
are now present with us, so Paul advises us to make a
deliberate effort to control (set) our minds on heavenly things
(3:2). If the navigator fails to set his sextant, his ship will
not reach the right port. Neither will an irresolute Christian
become mature or reach the destination God has planned
for him or her. Christ is in heaven, and since we are joined
to Him, our desires should be where He is (3:1). We are
pilgrims and strangers on earth, but are at home with Him
in heaven.

He is also "at home" (dwells) in Christians on earth.
What a wonderful association we have with Christ! This
association allows us to be close to God, because our old,
dead life is concealed (hidden) with Christ who is now "in
the bosom of the Father" (3:3; John 1:18).

Our resolve to sincerely desire heavenly things is of
primary importance. What do we *really* want—the sure things
above, or the uncertain things of earth? When one yearns
for God, worldly matters—materialism, laziness and pride—
will be left behind. Unless we firmly fix our intentions, we
will never experience the powerful, joyous lives God wants
us to have.

Paul, who was one of the strongest Christians, said,
"Even though the desire to do good is in me, I am not able
to do it. I don't do the good I want to do: instead I do the
evil I do not want to do" (Romans 7:18-19 TEV). This human condition made him feel wretched, but he relied on the
Holy Spirit to overcome his unstable behavior (Romans 8:13).

After we become Christians, God still does not violate
our wills but continues to allow us to make our own choices.
Within the souls of Christians there is continual warfare.
This conflict takes place where decisions are made and
emotions arise. We are tempted from without by the world
and the devil, and are haunted within by the ghosts of our
old, fleshly natures. When Christ "circumcised" us He removed and threw away our fleshly natures. But, because of

79

our shortsighted view of the future, we sometimes retrieve them from the garbage heap.

If our minds and wills are led by fleshly desires, we will fall. But if we allow Christ to lead from within, we will stand. Thus we see that the Christian life is the "inside-out" life of Christ influencing and acting from within until believers are "filled with all the fullness of God" (Ephesians 3:19).

Christ *is* the life of Christians (3:4). It isn't that He improves our *own* lives, but gives us *His* life. "He who has the Son has life" (1 John 5:12). It is God who works in us to cause us to *want* to do, and then to *do* what pleases Him (Philippians 2:13). Whatever we do that is of eternal value is done by His power, not ours. But we must cooperate with Him.

We are promised that when Christ returns we shall appear with Him in glory (3:4). Isn't that promise worth setting our minds on? Isn't that goal worth our continuing on in faith and not allowing ourselves to be moved from the hope of the Gospel (1:23)? Christ in us is truly our hope of glory! The best of Charlie's descendants from the earlier story couldn't give him such glory as that will be. No earthly reward can compare to being with Christ in glory!

Colossians 3:5-4:1 describes the kind of people God wants us to *be*, and the kinds of things He wants us to *do*. Notice that these instructions do not precede, but follow, the explanation of who Christ is and what He has done. God doesn't expect those who are not united with Christ to be and do what He asks of us here, although it is His will that every person come to know Christ and be changed. The key word in verses 5 and 12 is *therefore*, a word that refers to the statements of verses 3 and 4. That is, the believer's old life is dead and hidden in Christ, and Christ is his new life. That is the foundation of his ability to achieve the goals God has set for him.

The leaves of a diseased or insect-infested tree can only be pushed away and replaced by new foliage through action of the sap within the tree. In the same way, the attitudes and actions of the old life can only be removed and new, pure attitudes and actions be made to grow by the life of Christ within those who have received Him.

Colossians 3:5-11

Therefore put to death your members which are on the earth: fornication, uncleanness, passion, evil desire, and covetousness, which is idolatry. Because of these things the wrath of God is coming upon the sons of disobedience, in which you yourselves once walked when you lived in them.

But now you yourselves are to put off all these: anger, wrath, malice, blasphemy, filthy language out of your mouth. Do not lie to one another, since you have put off the old man with his deeds, and have put on the new man who is renewed in knowledge according to the image of Him who created him, where there is neither Greek nor Jew, circumcised nor uncircumcised, barbarian, Scythian, slave nor free, but Christ is all and in all.

Paul reminds the Colossians of what has already taken place in their lives; they have cast aside, or "taken off" the old sinful persons they used to be and have put on Christ (3:9-10). He compares the outward expressions of the new life within believers to putting on clothing (3:12). The garb of a prisoner is not appropriate for a prince. Neither are the trappings of sin suitable for a Christian. Therefore, Christians should divest themselves of all evil practices they once had. The very fact that Paul warns them, and us, about the dangers of holding on to the old life shows that it is possible for Christians to sin. We can be thankful that the blood of Christ continuously cleanses us from sin (1 John 1:7). Christians are not "new" only once, but are constantly being renewed and are gaining knowledge of God and Christ (3:10). We must remember, however, that if we deliberately keep on sinning after we have received the knowledge of the truth, we can expect only fearful judgment. To sin willfully is treating the blood of the cross as a common thing (Hebrews 10:26-31).

Verses 5, 8 and 9 list many attitudes and actions that are not heavenly, but earthly. Christians are to "mortify" or "put to death" these things. Paul is not telling the Colossians to execute members of their church who behave according to earthly standards. The New International Version uses this clearer translation: "Put to death, therefore, whatever belongs to your earthly natures." "This verb (put to death) occurs elsewhere, in the biblical Greek, only in Romans 4:19 and Hebrews 11:12; in both cases of Abraham's physical condition in old age. Its plain meaning is to reduce to a state of death, or like death, inoperative."[1]

Seven of the sins mentioned here are sins of attitude and emotions. They may be the cause of the four sins of behavior which are listed. Notice that covetousness, or greed, is called idolatry. Idolatry is the worship of anything or anyone except the one true God, the God of the Bible. Greed is the worship of oneself. Worship of humanity in any form, including self-worship, is the basis of all sin and rebellion against God. That is why greed is idolatry in unadulterated form.

Three of the acts of sin mentioned here are sins of the tongue. Jesus said, "A good man out of the good treasure of his heart brings forth good; and an evil man out of the evil treasure of his heart brings forth evil. For out of the abundance of the heart his mouth speaks" (Luke 6:45). An evil person might deceive his or her associates for a while, but eventually one's words or tone of voice will reveal the true nature overflowing from the heart.

Blasphemy is the worst use of words, for to blaspheme means "to speak against God."

It may be surprising to find that Christians need to be reminded not to lie to each other. In the Greek, the word *lie* is in the form which means "stop lying" (translation by Bob Hendren). Christians have the same temptations as others, including the temptation to lie.

The fourth sin mentioned here is fornication. Fornication is "all male or female indulgence of lust, including adultery and incest."[2] In God's plan, sexual intercourse is not to be combined with lust, but with love and commitment. In the beginning He established that the relationship between husband and wife is to be maintained even above our blood relationship with parents. He said that husband

and wife should cleave (be glued) to each other (Genesis 2:24-25). He set up this rule because He made us, knows us, and loves us. He wants for us only what is best.

Today's news media report the unhappiness and suffering caused by fornication. The nation suffers a monumental financial cost for "family-planning" clinics, treatment of sexually transmitted diseases, and rearing and educating unwanted children. One sad result of illicit sex is homes where children are not being reared by their own two well-disciplined parents. Pregnancies out of wedlock sometimes lead to murder of infants, both before and after birth. Women engage in frenzied fights for the *right* to control their own bodies after pregnancy, but don't practice the *responsibility* of controlling their bodies earlier.

Young boys and girls who have received so-called sex "education" may avoid pregnancy and think they have escaped the consequences of promiscuity. But they have not. They have only trained themselves to shun enduring relationships. Sharing themselves with various sexual partners, they scatter pieces of their personalities here and there and never learn who they really are. If continued, fornication will destroy self-respect and cause those who practice it to hate their past and dread their future.

Remember that Paul is writing to Christians. Today's Christians also need these warnings. Parents should not only set good examples, but help their children resist Satan's enticements, including, "Everybody's doing it." Some of the "everybodies" in this case are the most glamorous, most popular public figures. But God's way must not be compromised. He instructs us to be self-controlled and chaste (Titus 2:5). The original word for "chaste" is sometimes translated "sacred."

Young people need to be taught the difference between physical and emotional attraction and dedicated love. A moment of indulging in lust can steal away forever the opportunity for a happy, loving relationship of a lifetime.

The purposes of God's good gift of sexual intercourse include not only the propagation of the human race, but the bonding of husband and wife. When practiced within God's design, sex preserves and strengthens marriages by helping couples to know and understand each other. It teaches them how to give. It brings pleasure, comfort, relaxation and joy. A growing, mature sex life nurtures a oneness that refreshes and rejoins a husband and wife who were first joined together by God.

In verse 6, a severe warning is given to those who continue to be disobedient at heart: they will be the objects of God's wrath. The wrath of God is terrifying and is deserved by those who rebel against letting the goodness of God change. May each of us be the object of only God's goodness and not of His wrath!

Everyone who puts on Christ has the same opportunity to be renewed and to know Him (3:10-11). People who are in Christ are in the place where there are no distinctions between races, social standing, or education. In Christ, their former religion doesn't matter; to them He is all things, and He is in all who are in Him (3:11). "If Christ is not all in your life, He is nothing."[3]

As we learned from the first chapter of Colossians, Christ has the supremacy in all things because of His resurrection. He now has the honor of sitting at God's right hand. This exalted position cannot be shared; that is the way things are. If anyone allows something or someone, including himself, to usurp Christ's rightful place in his heart, he has not altered reality. He has only thrown his own life out of kilter because he has removed himself from the true foundation of life.

Just as Christ carried His cross to be crucified on, so should we deny self and daily take up our crosses for the purpose of having the fleshly, earthly desires of our old natures put to death (Luke 9:23). No one can crucify himself or herself, for although all other limbs may be nailed down, the one last hand holding the hammer remains free. Only by submitting to the life of Christ within can we have victory over the flesh.

The rest of this chapter in Colossians tells about our high estate and the lowly attitude such a position demands.

Questions
1. List the ways in which the Colossian letter says that Christians are different from the persons they had been (1:12-14, 22, 27; 2:10-13, 20; 3:1, 3-4, 12, 15, 24).
2. As a Christian, do you feel different? Does your feeling change God's Word of truth (1 John 5:13)?

3. How does one's opinion of himself affect his or her behavior?
4. How does a Christian's knowledge of Christ affect his or her behavior?
5. Which is more important to a Christian's daily life—his opinion of himself, or his knowledge of Christ?
6. Is there hope for believers who don't always think and behave as they should (Psalm 51:1-17; James 4:6-10; Psalm 86:5)?

Chapter 10

Colossians 3:12-17

This portion of Paul's letter deals with relationships in the church. God gave each believer a measure of faith (Romans 12:3). Embryonic though it may have been at the beginning, it caused us to trust the saving power of Jesus Christ. His divine power now within Christians can continue to save us daily. It has given us everything we need for life and godliness. God has given us great and precious promises so that we may be partakers of the divine nature and escape worldly, lustful corruption (2 Peter 1:3-4).

So we see again that God asks us to do what can be done only by the Holy Spirit which He gave us when we first became Christians. In Ephesians 5:18, Paul writes that Christians should be *filled* with the Spirit—that is, not once only, but repeatedly be under His influence as the occasion requires.[1]

Colossians 3:12-14

Therefore, as the elect of God, holy and beloved, put on tender mercies, kindness, humility, meekness, longsuffering; bearing with one another, and forgiving one another, if anyone has a complaint against another; even as Christ forgave you, so you also must do. But above all these things put on love, which is the bond of perfection.

By His grace, believers are "the elect of God, holy, and beloved." This is who God says we are. It is only normal that our lives produce appropriate expressions of who we are. In the original, the word for "elect" means "those who are selected." In no way does the word imply the rejection of others. It means that, as a favor, God selects Christians in the same way He chose the nation of Israel to be His. Without rejecting other individuals, He chose Israel because He loved them (Deuteronomy 7:7-8).

In saying Christians are "holy," He means that they have "come out" from the world. They are sacred in God's sight and "set apart" to be pure.

The word *beloved* means that Christians have received God's love, not because of what we were, but in spite of what we were.[2]

We have read the negative characteristics Paul told us to "take off" (3:8). Now he tells us the traits with which we should clothe ourselves. The clothing Paul tells us to wear is not a "put-on" or pretense. It actually portrays one who has first put on Christ (Galatians 3:27). The robes of royalty he wants Christians to wear are listed in verses 12-14. They are not synthetic, theatrical costumes that are temporary, unbecoming, and don't wear well. They are the 100% wool, pure silk, 24-karat gold garments of those who are aware that they are dearly loved by God. Yet, these royal robes are also the uniform of service (3:14).

The listed characteristics—tender mercies (compassion), kindness (sweet sympathy), humbleness of mind, meekness, and longsuffering—may appear to be expressions of weakness. In reality, they belong only to the strong. It is impossible for those who don't know God's love to have these traits, for they are not products of fallen human nature. They come from God alone.

Those who are compassionate are tenderly alert to the feelings of others. Humbleness of mind causes us to honestly compare ourselves with others and with Christ. "The phrase 'humbleness of mind' is not older in Greek than the New Testament, and the grace is essentially Christian, the attitude of a soul which has lost its pride in its discovery of the mercy of its salvation."[3]

Christ's humility caused Him to leave heaven, become human and endure death by crucifixion. Gentleness, or *meekness*, is "strength under control." That is, it is strength used for the right purposes and in the right way. In the original language, *longsuffering* or *patience* means "long passion," or to feel deeply, with lasting empathy (translations by Bob Hendren).

God loves the unlovely and has placed all kinds of believers in Christ's body together. None of us deserves His love. Therefore, we are told to "bear with" (put up with) one another. One might say, "Tolerance is a poor substitute for love." Tolerance is also one way to demonstrate love. Each of us needs to be put up with at times, so it is only fair and right that we be lenient with others. Paul also says that if any member has a legitimate complaint against another, he should forgive him. This statement implies that the harmed Christian doesn't harbor his hurt feelings, but tells those who have injured him.

The reason for forgiving others is because the Lord forgave us (3:13). Decisions about forgiving should not be based on "Does this person deserve forgiveness?" or "Has this person ever forgiven me?" The criterion for forgiving is "The Lord forgave me."

When I was a child in the 1920s, new high-topped shoes came with my mother's instruction, "Keep the strings tied or you'll step on their tips, break them and make it difficult to put them through the eyelets." Having done exactly what I'd been told not to do, rather than tell my mother, I once wrestled for two days, trying to push the frayed ends through the eyelets. One morning, about to be late for school and needing help, I was forced to admit what I'd done.

Imagine my surprise when my mother answered, "I've been wondering when you'd tell me. The day we bought the shoes I got extra laces and have kept them ready until you asked for them."

Christ's forgiveness is always present. It was ready and waiting long before we first repented and asked to be forgiven. He continues to have an inexhaustible supply of forgiveness and "shoelaces" which He gives us for a fresh start when we ask for them. Therefore, simply because He forgave us, we too should constantly be forgiving of our fellow Christians, whether or not they ask to be forgiven.

A situation of having to forgive demonstrates that *being* is more important than *doing*. Without saying or doing a single thing, a Christian can *be* forgiving. A Christian who has been mistreated has opportunity to discover whether he or she is the kind of person who will "turn the other cheek" (Matthew 5:39).

In verse 14, Paul uses a familiar image of his day: a cord tied around the waist was used to tuck in the skirts of their long, loose garments when the wearer needed to move freely for active work. In the same way, love is the girdle or belt that binds all these virtues together and makes them workable and effective. The awareness that God loves both us and all others in the church frees us to express His love and ours. An affectation of concern won't work. Genuine love will.

Perhaps there is someone you don't yet love. Go to God, and with faith ask for love for that person. God wants to give us love for others, and if we truly believe, He will answer that prayer for love. Therefore, you can treat that person as you would treat anyone you love, because you do love him. Jesus promised in Mark 11:24, "Whatever you ask for in prayer, *believe* that you *have received* it and it will be yours" (New English Bible). If you sincerely believe you have already received love for that person, then treating him or her with love becomes an honest act.

Colossians 3:15-17

And let the peace of God rule in your hearts, to which also you were called in one body; and be thankful. Let the word of Christ dwell in you richly in all wisdom, teaching and admonishing one another in psalms and hymns and spiritual songs, singing with grace in your hearts to the Lord. And whatever you do in word or deed, do all in the name of the Lord Jesus, giving thanks to God the Father through Him.

These three verses tell of the importance of practices that are often thought to be mere form or ritual. On the contrary, these practices contribute to the unity and growth of the church. They also tell of the power of peace.

Often we think of peace as being like a quiet pool. But here we are told that Christ's peace should rule, or "preside," as that word means. We can conclude, then, that Christ's peace is a strong, active, controlling force. Rather than being a still pool, it is a gentle eddy running contrary to the world, pulling aside all those attracted to its slow but strong swirl (3:15). His peace is constant but never stagnant. Graciously and surely, it draws to Him and to each other all those who allow it to do so.

It is not normal for Christians to resist peace. Yet, we do oppose it, returning again and again to the downstream rapids of dissension and turmoil. Sometimes it prevents us from genuinely accepting a brother or sister whom God accepts.

These traits of Christians are not listed here for the purpose of judging or "grading" others. They are to be used for honest self-evaluation. When *I* am ruled by peace I can "put up with" and be compassionate and understanding of others in God's church who may have more reason than I to resist peace. Individual personality, as well as childhood environment, has a strong influence on how fearful each adult may be. Parents that are cold or that speak gruffly cause a child to be wary of the reactions of everyone. A child that has been physically or emotionally abused may live an entire lifetime of fear unless he or she comes to know the love of Christ and the peace it brings.

Competitive people sometimes get their "kicks" from neighborhood arguments, lawsuits, or at least by verbal "put-downs." This way of life is a habit that is difficult to break. As Christians, we can enjoy mature "inside-out" living and leave behind adolescent squabbles if we allow Christ's peace to rule in our hearts.

Paul didn't expect the Colossian Christians to be the kind of people God wanted them to be without letting the Word of Christ live in them richly. They did not have such a large supply of His Word as we do today. Although there was not as much available, it could be in them richly if each one knew it. Thus, by teaching and admonishing each other, they attained this wealth of knowledge of God's Word (3:16). What we hear or read shouldn't lie dormant in our minds, but should be shared.

God's Word is living, active and productive (Hebrews 4:12). The method of teaching mentioned here is singing. More fully than other creatures, mankind can combine music and language to express the thoughts and feelings of his heart. What a joy it is to do this "unto God" with whatever voice or ear for melody He has given us!

The positive *attitudes* Christians should wear have been dealt with first because only by having the right attitudes can we *do* the right things. We are told that everything we do should be done "in the name of the Lord Jesus" (3:17). This phrase asserts that it should be done by His authority and power, like an ambassador representing his country.

Gnostics taught that each person's deeds were authenticated by or done "in the name of" an angel. Some angels were of higher rank than others, so the person whose angel was of highest rank supposedly had the most power. The Lord Jesus outranks all angels and all others. He is called "Lord" here, and if we consider Him Lord, we will not try to misuse His authority.

One must have a rich knowledge of the Word of Christ before he claims to be acting in Christ's name. If our lives are running smoothly or we are financially prosperous, it is not necessarily true that we are acting by the authority of Christ. Neither does a feeling of pleasure or happiness always indicate we are acting according to His will. "I must be doing something right" is not always the correct conclusion. Personally knowing Christ and His Word is the only way to safeguard against being deceived by feelings. Christ does not authenticate actions which are contrary to the Bible.

Each person is different and has different experiences. No book is large enough to contain all the applications this chapter may have in the lives of many different people. God has told us many times before how to live. Since the Garden of Eden, He has told us by precept, historical illustrations, and the example of Christ's life. A human father might say in anger, "If I've told you once I've told you a thousand times to do thus and so!" But our heavenly Father is patient. He kindly but ardently repeats His advice and warns us of the consequences of disobedience.

God is gracious and forgiving when we repent; that gives us even more reason not to attempt to take advantage of His love. As impure as *we* are, we dislike being abused because we are willing to forgive. The *holy God* has every right to be angry when we take His forgiveness for granted.

Let us pray we won't "push our luck" and make trial of Him by ignoring Him.

When we disobey, He is saddened—because He loves us and has given His all for us (Romans 5:8; 2 Peter 3:9). He wants us to be close to Him, so we should accept His divine continued invitations to remain there. Sin separates us from God, and we can become disastrously and eternally hardened in heart and "crucify the Son of God all over again" (Isaiah 59:1-2; Hebrews 6:4-6 NIV). God is slow to anger, but He will not always merely reprove (Psalm 103:8-9).

Who knows how we function best? The inventor of a machine knows what it is to be used for, how to use it, and how to maintain it. We are much more complex than any machine. God, our Maker, knows better what is good for us than an inventor knows his machine. In addition, God loves us; He will never give harmful instructions. If we trust Him, He will also supply the motivation and ability to follow His instructions. He can even guard us from stumbling as long as we depend upon Him (Jude 24-25).

Unity results when all members of the body know the Word of Christ and follow it. He is head of the body; His purpose is not divided; He does not vacillate in His precepts and decisions for the church and its members.

Three times in this paragraph, gratitude is mentioned. For the peace of Christ, in verse 15, we are told to be thankful. If we are grateful to God for everything He has done, we will find peace within our own being, and we will be at peace with others. In verse 16, we are told to sing with grace, or gratitude, in our hearts. A song that doesn't come from a grateful heart is merely a performance, not true worship.

In verse 17, we are told that our words and actions should come from a grateful heart. Gratitude takes the drudgery out of serving, replacing it with joy. If we let it be known that it is only by the grace of God that we are able to serve, people would never disdain us as being hypocritical "do-gooders." If they see an attitude of gratitude in us when we do good works, they would not glorify us, but our Father who is in heaven (Matthew 5:16).

Instructions about relationships in the family are found in the succeeding verses and will be discussed in the next chapter.

93

Questions

1. Why should Christians have a *rich* knowledge of the Bible?
2. Do non-Christians think professed Christians should be representatives of the Lord? Can a Christian be a false representative of the Lord?
3. List instances when being grateful to God has helped you. In what ways has it helped you?
4. What are your reasons for obeying God?
5. Of the Christian attitudes mentioned in Colossians 3:12-14, which are the most difficult for you to attain?

Chapter 11

Colossians 3:18-21

In our relationships with people, the basis for our behavior should be our relationship with God. A person must be right with God before he can begin to be right with others (Ephesians 5:21). Being right with God means giving up one's own will for Christ's sake (Matthew 10:39). Only by first submitting to Christ can we submit to others, as He submitted to others (1 Peter 2:21-23).

In the above verses, wives are reminded of what is *fitting in the Lord.* Children are told about what *pleases the Lord.*

Colossians 3:18-19

Wives, submit to your own husbands, as is fitting in the Lord. Husbands, love your wives and do not be bitter toward them.

Just as in other decisions, in America each person has the freedom to choose whether he or she will marry or remain single. But God has provided marriage as the way for a man and woman to live together happily. In the beginning He said, "It isn't good for man to be alone," and made a companion for Adam.

Being married doesn't ensure happiness. Since Paul knows personally only two people from Colosse, we assume that he isn't giving individual counseling here. Verses 18 and 19 are a capsule edition of instructions for marriage partners. But his words, inspired by the Holy Spirit, are true. He gives the Colossians, and us, some fundamentals that, if observed, will support strong and loving homes. It is appropriate for wives to submit to their husbands because the husband *is* (not merely should be) the head of the wife (Ephesians 5:23). Husband and wife should each assume his or her role and avoid creating a two-headed monster.

In the original language, the word *submit* means "to place under." The husband is not told to place his wife in this position—the wife is to place herself there. A husband and wife are equally capable of performing their respective roles, but God's plan is that they not play the same role. Try as they may, men cannot be women; women cannot be men. Whatever the circumstances may be, at best they can only be substitutes for the opposite sex.

A husband is head of the wife in the same way that Christ is head of the church (Ephesians 5:23). Since the responsibility of leadership is his, fairness and wisdom demand that his wife work with him, not against him. It is even possible for a wife to convert a non-Christian husband without "preaching" (1 Peter 3:1).

A wife was created for the purpose of being a helper for her husband (Genesis 2:18). She does this best when she doesn't usurp his authority. A woman who is complete in Christ can express her own desires, encourage and inspire her mate, and warn him of dangers in ways that are helpful. But if she habitually and independently makes decisions for the family, her husband cannot become a wise leader. She should plan with her husband, and then, as a rule, wait for his decisions.

There are, however, legitimate exceptions to this rule. In the case of a husband's poor health it may be impossible for him to make decisions. If he is absent and unavailable, and when emergencies arise, a wife must have complete authority. It is best for her to have experience in decision-making before it becomes a necessity. Even if unauthorized by her husband, there are some things a wife must do to please God.

One of these activities is to teach the Bible to her children. This is done more successfully when both parents participate, but in any case, must not be neglected. We don't know whether Timothy's Gentile father took part in his son's religious training. But Paul congratulated Timothy's Jewish mother and grandmother because their faith was a major influence on this young Christian. Since faith is based on hearing God's Word, we may assume that these two women taught Timothy the Old Testament scriptures and that Jesus is the Messiah spoken of there. Under no circumstances should a wife delay this vital teaching of the Gospel.

In telling husbands to love their wives, Paul uses the Greek word for *love* that is used to describe God's love. It is self-sacrificing love. It is love for the unlovely. It is love for one who doesn't deserve love. How can we have the same kind of love God has? The Holy Spirit puts God's love into our hearts; with His help, we can express that love (Romans 5:5).

Ephesians 5:21-33 gives a fuller explanation of the relationship husbands and wives should have first with Christ, then with each other. Prayerfully read this passage now. It shows that a husband should assume his position as leader, but is not to lord it over his family in a dictatorial way. His is to be a life of service to his wife as Christ's life is to the church, while hers is to be one of helping her husband. A husband and wife are dependent upon each other and will solidify their marriage by showing each other, "I need you." Those three little words have lifted the heart of many a spouse.

Neither the Ephesian nor the Colossian passage mentions that a husband or wife should reciprocate love "in kind." "He or she doesn't love me" is not a scriptural reason for not loving. Environment and training influence our methods of showing love. At times husbands and wives may not show love in the way their spouses would want. Sometimes they may not show love at all. The most anyone can expect of a spouse is that each show love to the best of his or her ability.

Some spouses show love by showering gifts on their mates, while others do the same by helping with chores, building up their partner's self-respect, by being dependable, or by being frugal. Some spouses may never forget birthdays and anniversaries. Others never remember a spouse's mistakes and faults.

But a husband or wife should expect a spouse never to act in ways that demonstrate an absence of love. Both men and women can be unfaithful or become physically and psychologically abusive. These actions may be caused by a faulty personality or by physical or emotional illness. When these things occur, a spouse should let it be known affably, but firmly and directly, that such behavior will not be tolerated. If both husband and wife determine to submit to Christ, to act only in love, and to forgive, they can make a new start.

Sadly, this doesn't always happen. When any couple, including Christians, are trying to mend their marriage, improvement will not be automatic. Only prayer and effort bring lasting improvement. It is helpful for both parties to seek spiritual and emotional counsel from a trusted, competent, praying person who knows God. If one partner refuses to do this, the other should consult a counselor alone.

Asking for help is not a sign of weakness, but is a practical remedial thing to do. Postponing taking such positive action can only make matters worse. If a husband and wife are honest with themselves and with each other, a capable third person can lead them to discover the causes of their problems. Then solutions can be worked out. Difficulties in marriage demand difficult decisions. Each marriage is different; each person is different; solutions must be different.

The best way to avoid marital troubles is to avoid unhappy marriages. Today's fast pace can become a habit, ensnare us and pull us into hasty decisions to marry too quickly.

Courting usually takes place at an age when desire for independence from parents and physical attraction for the opposite sex are strong. When dating, being human, we are careful to show only our best side. Dates are times of fun and recreation—not of discussion of differences in the philosophies of two people.

Just to know your sweetheart's likes and dislikes, or even his or her economic and educational background, is not enough. Each person's understanding of marriage has been formed mainly by experience with his or her parents. A better criteria for a good marriage is what the Bible teaches about it. A good beginning for sweethearts considering marriage is to study it together.

People embarking on a lifetime together—and that is what God designed it to be—should know each other well enough to ask and give honest answers to straightforward, thoughtful questions. Ask what is important to you. Some questions might be: "Describe love and what it does"; "What are the differing roles of husband and wife?"; "Do you want children, and whose responsibility is child-rearing?"; and "What do you pray about?"

When either party is widowed, and especially if either of them has children, these questions are doubly important. A bad marriage is no solution to child care. Neither is it a solution to loneliness.

Life is difficult when one must associate with those whose thinking is different from ours, whether it be at work, in school, or at recreation. The most disastrous circumstance of "unequal yoking" is marriage. Paul, when writing to Christians in the pagan city of Corinth, warns against such a liaison (2 Corinthians 6:14-16).

The decision to take a lifetime partner demands much prayer, then waiting for, recognizing, and obeying God's answer. With faith in Christ, and with the willingness to mature, men and women can find deep happiness and lasting fulfillment in marriage, a relationship designed by God. Other scriptures about marriage and divorce are 1 Peter 3:1-7; 1 Corinthians 7; and Matthew 19:3-12.

Instructions to Children and Parents
Colossians 3:20-21

Children, obey your parents in all things, for this is well pleasing to the Lord. Fathers, do not provoke your children, lest they become discouraged.

God honors us by entrusting to us His highest creation—children whose souls will live forever. These precious beings are presented to us in a physically weak, helpless and charming state. Yet they possess the God-given privilege of becoming masters of their own fate.

To successfully guide this inner drive of infants to wisely take command of their own lives is the challenge given parents. With God's help, the weak can become strong, the helpless can become helper, and the charm will remain and will show itself in practical ways.

Evidently, Paul's advice to the children of Colosse is for those old enough to have a desire to please the Lord (3:20). We will discuss this instruction first, along with that given parents. Then we will study how very young children may be led to want to please God.

Paul tells children to obey both parents in all things. One might ask, "In everything?" Choosing which rules to follow and which to ignore is obedience only to oneself and to one's own will. Respect for authority is essential to living a happy life. A healthy regard for authority is best learned in childhood. Disobedience to parents can develop into a lifetime of rebellion against God. The only scriptural exception to this rule of obedience to parents is when a decision must be made between obedience to God and obedience to humans (Matthew 10:37; Acts 5:29).

The word *obey* here is a strong one. "The wife 'submits herself' as to a guiding friend; the child and servant (3:22) recognize in parent and master a lawful commander."[1] The importance of obedience to parents is shown in the way God told Israel to deal with disobedient sons (Deuteronomy 21:18-21).

In writing, "children, obey your parents in all things," Paul paints the ideal picture of non-competitive parents agreeing on what their children should obey. If the authority of one parent is undermined, the foundation of their children's lives is weakened. Therefore, parents must be careful when disagreeing. If one parent implies to the child, "*I* am your friend," the child will assume that the other is his enemy. It is best for parents to discuss their differences in private before giving directives. Then they can support each other and lay a strong groundwork for life.

Often parents are tempted by the "cuteness" of their toddlers to delay building on that strong base. They should look at wild horses who may enjoy their high-spirited freedom as they gambol and gallop on the range. But their short, vulnerable lives of irresponsibility don't compare with the care and safety that is theirs once they are bridled. When trained, their lives are long, healthy and useful.

In the same way, children that are guided in the right way can become happy, productive citizens. The task of parents is to lead them to be self-controlled and to accept the bridle of God's loving commandments. But parents must remember that children, made in God's image, are not horses.

Discipline must be instilled in the right way. Verse 21 states that fathers—this word can also be rendered "parents"—must not provoke their children. Unkindness might cause them to be discouraged, or "have a broken spirit" as that word means. Of all the rules Paul might have written to parents, he chose the important one not to discourage their children. Good parents will chasten their children when necessary (Proverbs 3:11-12).

Feeling the weight of their responsibility, parents may speak harshly to their children, or deal with them so severely that the children will be unable to achieve their goals. To them, it seems that their parents don't love them; and if they believe that their parents don't love them, how can they love themselves?

A parent who has strong guilt feelings often has difficulty reprimanding a child, especially when discipline requires punishment. Such guilt feelings can cause a parent to be either too lax and never punish, or to punish too severely. Parents must rely upon God to help them distinguish between the child's guilt and their own. When parents make mistakes of any kind in rearing their children, they should confess them to their children and to God, then accept the forgiveness of both.

Many dedicated parents worry that they are not teaching their children. But, for good or bad, they *are* teaching them. Parents are the first and foremost teachers of their children. That is why being good examples for our children is important. Learning begins when a baby, at its mother's breast, stares into her eyes, deeply scrutinizing. If affinity isn't broken, learning continues through adulthood as that offspring from time to time casts an analytical eye toward his or her parents.

Deuteronomy 6:6-9 specifies that teaching children about God should not be done only at set-aside times. It should be a daily way of life. Today, many children spend most of their waking hours with persons other than their parents. Those care-givers do most of the teaching. Choosing these helpers should be done prayerfully.

Deciding whether to delegate this solemn responsibility to others should be seriously and carefully thought out. For exactly what reasons are parents missing this pleasurable and important time with their children?

Training their children is the primary career of both father and mother. But as a result of sad misfortune or having made the mistake of ignoring God's instructions for a happy home, it is sometimes necessary for both parents to work. Unfortunately, this may be the case even during those few short years when a child learns fastest—those years before the law requires a child to spend most of his or her time in school.

Do both parents work in order to have the necessities of life? Or is it that they agree with the profiteers who saturate our minds with the notion that many extras are necessities? Actively participating in this lie that one's life consists in the abundance of the things one possesses forces parents to sacrifice time with their children—time that can never be regained.

To do this undermines their children's self-esteem. Parents who are taken in, along with their children, by television commercials and drama demonstrate by example that personal value is dependent upon the price and popularity of the things one owns. Working to buy unnecessary things also teaches children to be self-indulgent.

What did the parents of Colosse do to "prepare the soil" of the hearts of their young children to receive the "seed" of the Word of God? Following are suggestions of what they may have taught. Teaching these important things takes time, thought and prayer as parents come to know each individual child.

As soon as children can speak a phrase, most parents wisely teach them to say "thank you." This little ritual can become sincere *gratitude* to God, which is the basic response to Him that dictates our relationship with Him.

A very small child can become "*God conscious.*" This awareness of God's presence can be taught by example if we show, as well as tell, that God is real to us. We should not be shy about praying in front of our children—we should pray with them rather than just "hear" their goodnight prayers. A child's first sensation of God can grow into a realization of Him like that of Job's. In spite of severe trials, Job never failed to declare that there is a God who was involved in his life.

Encouraging children to express their thoughts and feelings about everything, especially about Jesus, can help them to have *faith in God*, but only if they can trust their parents. Children learn in early childhood whether or not to trust. Children who can rely on the word of their parents are more likely to believe God's Word. Being inconsistent and changeable in what one expects of a child is frustrating to him or her. Therefore, parents must be careful when setting boundaries and making promises. Parents who don't keep their promises are not providing for them a firm foundation for life. By example, they are also teaching them to lie.

As we have learned, *love of the truth* is crucial. A child who has been trained to know the difference between his own imagination (which should not be squelched) and what really happens grows up to be realistic. This realism helps him or her to manage personal finances, to advance in a career, and to wisely choose a mate. Without it, a person cannot learn the relation between cause and effect. Most importantly, the heart of an honest child is the "good soil" which receives and understands God's Word (Matthew 13:23).

It is imperative that we give our children *Bible knowledge*. Later in life, when exposed to the philosophies of the world, their faith may waver, and for a while they may depart from God's way. We still cannot force them to think like we do. As adults, they are not responsible to us, but to God Himself. But, if when they were children we gave them an understanding of the good news of the cross, we can know that it continues to draw them to Christ (John 12:23).

If we had been putting the future of the human race in the hands of individuals, we may have chosen middle-aged, experienced people. But God wisely gives children to young people who have much to learn. Can parents learn from infants and toddlers who have come to us unmarred by the world? Yes, we can learn refreshing, reviving ways of life.

We can learn to *express emotion*—to laugh when happy, to cry when sad. Although children must learn what is and what is not theirs, they are happiest when sharing. We can learn again from them that it is more blessed *to give* than to receive.

103

From children we can learn *to forgive*. They tend to forget bad experiences, unless frequently repeated. They don't hold grudges, but forgive much like God forgives. His forgiveness is constant and strengthens and revitalizes us as we perform the delightful duties of nurturing these precious souls.

Guiding and training children is difficult, but it brings joy. Solomon said, "A wise son makes a glad father," and adds that the children of a worthy woman rise up and call her blessed (Proverbs 10:1; 31:28).

Questions

1. After committing adultery with Bathsheba and ordering Uriah to be killed, whom did David feel his primary sin was against (Psalm 51:4)?
2. How can a couple make a wise decision about getting married (James 1:5)?
3. Why does what one prays about reveal his or her nature? What does it tell us about ourselves?
4. Should Christians confess their sins to members of their own family? Is that less difficult than confessing to other people?
5. Why must parents behave honorably (Exodus 20:12)?
6. If we aren't thankful to God, what kind of people might we become (Romans 1:12)?
7. What must family members do in order to have a happy home (Colossians 3:12-13)?
8. What is the overall attitude necessary to make child-rearing and family life successful (Colossians 3:14)?

Chapter 12

Colossians 3:22-4:18

Paul continues to give advice about Christians' relationships with others. First, he speaks of their conduct and attitude in the workplace. Then he instructs the church at Colosse about how to deal with non-Christians. In the last eleven verses he demonstrates the interest and feeling we should have for other Christians, even when we don't know them personally.

Instructions to Masters and Servants
Colossians 3:22-4:1

Bondservants, obey in all things your masters according to the flesh, not with eyeservice, as men-pleasers, but in sincerity of heart, fearing God. And whatever you do, do it heartily, as to the Lord and not to men, knowing that from the Lord you will receive the reward of the inheritance; for you serve the Lord Christ. But he who does wrong will be repaid for what he has done, and there is no partiality.

Masters, give your bondservants what is just and fair, knowing that you also have a Master in heaven.

These principles for servants and the masters who owned them apply today to employees and employers. If only they could be followed, labor troubles would be solved before they became unmanageable; indeed, they might never arise.

Whether the Colossian masters were Christians and the slaves were not, or if the situation was reversed, the relationship was to be the same. These men were masters in the economic rather than the spiritual world, for both master and servant had a Master in heaven whether or not they accepted Him as such (3:22; 4:1).

Servants—then and now—are not to give eye-service, merely trying to get by. People who work for others should not be men-pleasers, or "apple-polishers." They are to have the same purpose as their employers.

Paul gives no involved explanations as to why servants should obey their masters; it is for the simple reason that they do right for right's sake. They are to work in sincerity of heart, or "out from the soul" as the expression means in the Greek, because their real Master is the Lord for whom they should have respect. The Lord Himself is the one who will reward both master and servant, perhaps in this life, but surely in the life to come. He will give them the reward or punishment deserved for their dealings with each other. God is impartial to both employer and employee.

Doing whatever we do in the work place "as unto the Lord" is living by the principle of "doing all in the name of the Lord." Working "as unto the Lord" lightens any burden and brings joy to any task.

In the happiest times of marriage, childhood, parenting, and vocation this joy is the "icing on the cake." During times of trial, whether with spouse, children, parents or those with whom we work, doing everything as unto the Lord becomes our meat and drink. That is, the constant awareness of our relationship with God is what sustains us and causes us to grow. Whether times were smooth or rough, doing God's will was Jesus' meat (John 4:34). When we learn to honestly and continually say, "Nevertheless, not my will but thine be done," then we will know real joy.

From the third chapter of Colossians we have learned that the powerful life is the submitted life—submission to God and to others. Jesus was victorious over every situation of life and victorious over death because He yielded to God's will. We, too, can be triumphant if we practice the paradox of victory through submission. But first, we must sincerely determine that wherever submitting may take us, we *shall* keep our minds set on eternal things (3:2).

Colossians 4:2-6

> Continue earnestly in prayer, being vigilant in it with thanksgiving; meanwhile praying also for us, that God would open to us a door for the word, to speak the mystery of Christ, for which I am also in chains, that I may make it manifest, as I ought to speak.
>
> Walk in wisdom toward those who are outside, redeeming the time. Let your speech always be with grace, seasoned with salt, that you may know how you ought to answer each one.

These five verses give two main points about the body of Christ:

1. The importance of prayer to the life of the church; and
2. The importance of the message of the church.

Paul expected the devotions of the heart and actions of a busy life to take place within the same Christian. God seldom prescribes that some persons devote their whole lives to prayer, while others devote their lives only to service. When prayer is sincere it will lead to service. For service to be effective, it must be accompanied by prayer. We read here that dedicated prayer for oneself and others progresses to a wise lifestyle and gracious speech.

We shouldn't think that Christian conduct occurs automatically simply because we are in Christ and Christ is in us. As long as we are in the world as well as in Christ, we must strive to submit to Christ rather than to the earthly things that tempt us. Prayer is necessary.

When Paul tells us to pray, he doesn't mean an occasional "reaching out and touching" God when we are in special need or when we are particularly thankful. He says we should give constant attention to prayer, or "continue earnestly," as some translations read, and that we should be vigilant (watchful) as we pray. We should watch for dangers to our souls, and we should watch especially for God's answers to prayer. In that way, we can keep up-to-date in our petitions and our thanksgivings, and we will recognize opportunities for prayer and service.

Prayer is a "two-way radio," but often words aren't necessary for communication. A consciousness of God's presence fills us; we cannot enjoy a blessing or a moment of joy without our thanksgiving going to Him. "True trust in God is constantly crystallizing into definite prayer to God." Prayer is not merely urging our wishes on God. "True prayer is the meeting in harmony of God's will and man's, and its deepest expression is not, 'Do this, because I desire it, O Lord; but I do this because Thou desirest it, O Lord.'"[1]

Paul also asks for the prayers of the Colossian Christians on behalf of himself and those who are with him. He asks humbly, but without apology, since he knows how important their prayers are—both to him and to them. Praying for him will give them one more opportunity to communicate with their Father.

The importance of what Paul asks them to pray for is another reason for them to pray: that a door for the Word will be opened. Only "He who is holy, He who is true" has power to "open and no one shuts, and shuts and no one opens" (Revelation 3:7). The most thorough campaigns, the most entertaining speakers, and the most elaborate programs will not open a single heart, for only God can accomplish that.

At another time Paul asked for prayers "that the word of the Lord may spread rapidly and be honored" (2 Thessalonians 3:1). Teaching about the mystery of Christ had put Paul in prison, not once, but many times (4:3; 2 Corinthians 11:23). Although he was in prison at this time, he didn't ask that prison doors be opened, but that doors of opportunity for God's Word be opened. And although he remained incarcerated, the prayers were answered. For centuries God has opened hearts to the message Paul wrote from prison. The lessons he taught Mark and Luke, who were with him during his imprisonment, continue to influence others.

Since the Colossian church, as well as Paul, would come in contact with people who didn't know the message of Christ, Paul advised them on how they should conduct themselves toward "those who are outside"—those who were not in Christ. When He sent the apostles to preach, Jesus told them to be "wise as serpents and harmless as doves."

Christians are still like "sheep in the midst of wolves," so wisdom is very much needed if we are to influence others to accept Christ (Matthew 10:16). But the message of Christ must not be postponed. Will there be a tomorrow?

Paul tells how Christians should speak (4:6). He says our speech should always be gracious, and that it should be "seasoned with salt." If we are sincerely thankful for undeserved blessings from God, our speech will be full of grace and humility.

The incense which burned on the golden altar in the tabernacle was seasoned with salt. God told those who worshiped there, "You shall not make any [incense] for yourselves ... It shall be to you holy for the Lord (Exodus 30:34-37)." When our words are seasoned with salt, they, too, are an oblation to God. They influence those outside Christ. Salt preserves and gives flavor. Our speech should contain words of salvation and be "flavorful." That means our speech should be interesting and contain words of salvation. If we talk about the needs and interests of those to whom we are speaking, our speech will be interesting to them. However, if we gain their attention yet never speak words of salvation, our speech is useless.

Colossians 4:7-18

Tychicus, a beloved brother, faithful minister, and fellow servant in the Lord, will tell you all the news about me. I am sending him to you for this very purpose, that he may know your circumstances and comfort your hearts, with Onesimus, a faithful and beloved brother, who is one of you. They will make known to you all things which are happening here.

Aristarchus my fellow prisoner greets you, with Mark the cousin of Barnabas (about whom you received instructions: if he comes to you, welcome him), and Jesus who is called Justus. These are my only fellow workers for the kingdom of God who are of the circumcision: they have proved to be a comfort to me.

Epaphras, who is one of you, a bondservant of Christ, greets you, always laboring fervently for you in prayers, that you may stand perfect and complete in all the will of God. For I bear him witness that he has a great zeal for you, and those who are in Laodicea, and those in Hierapolis. Luke the beloved physician and Demas greet you. Greet the brethren who are in Laodicea, and Nymphas and the church that is in his house.

Now when this epistle is read among you, see that it is read also in the church of the Laodiceans, and that you likewise read the epistle from Laodicea. And say to Archippus, "Take heed to the ministry which you have received in the Lord, that you may fulfill it."

This salutation by my own hand—Paul. Remember my chains. Grace be with you. Amen.

In these closing lines of the letter, Paul sends personal messages from his companions and himself. As we read we can feel the love between these Christians in Rome, Colosse and Laodicea. Paul calls them "beloved," "faithful," "ministers," "fellow-servants," "brothers," "fellow-prisoners," "servants of Christ Jesus," and a comfort to him. Epaphras, of Colosse, prayed so fervently for them that it is called "laboring." The men who were with Paul in Rome may have visited him, or in the case of some, lived with him during the time he was allowed to live in a private house while still a prisoner (Acts 28:30-31). During that time, he had a Roman guard and at times was chained to the guard. The trip from Rome to Colosse was long and difficult, but it was the only means of delivering this letter. Tychicus and Onesimus were assigned the task (4:7-9). Tychicus also delivered Paul's letter to the Ephesian church. He had been a helper to Paul since before the riot in Ephesus (Acts 19-20). He had been sent on other errands by Paul (Titus 3:12).

Onesimus was the runaway slave we read about in the letter to Philemon. He had been converted to Christ by

Paul's teaching and had become profitable to him (Philemon 11). But because Christians are law-abiding, Onesimus returned to his master, Philemon, with the letter Paul had written in his behalf. How thankful we are that God has preserved the Bible through the centuries by using such faithful people to record and deliver it!

The next three men Paul mentions were Jewish Christians who were with him (4:10-11). They each sent greetings to the church in Colosse. Aristarchus had been with Paul before the uprising in Ephesus, too, and he and Luke followed Paul to Rome at the time of Paul's imprisonment (Acts 27:2).

We read more about Mark than any of the others mentioned here. He was the writer of the Gospel of Mark. He was the son of Mary, to whose house Peter came when he was miraculously freed from jail (Acts 12). Mark went with Paul on one missionary journey, then left him for a while. He returned to minister to Paul when asked to do so (2 Timothy 4:11).

The third Jewish man, Jesus who was called Justus, is mentioned in the Bible only once. Simply by sending his well-wishes to other Christians, his name has been recorded in God's Word.

Epaphras was a member of the body at Colosse. In his letter to Philemon, Paul calls Epaphras his "fellow-prisoner."

The next two men Paul mentions are spiritual opposites. Luke was a close friend of Paul's. He was a physician. He wrote the Gospel of Luke and the Acts of the Apostles, in which he carefully recounts details of the life of Christ and events of the early church. Evidently, at this time Demas was still faithful. But in a later letter Paul wrote that Demas had deserted him because he "loved this present world." John tells us, "If anyone loves the world, the love of the Father is not in him" (1 John 2:15). This reference shows that association with Christians doesn't necessarily keep one's faith firm. Each person's relationship with God is an individual matter. We read nothing more about Demas, but we do know that if he confessed his sin, God, who is faithful and just to forgive our sins, cleansed him from all unrighteousness (1 John 1:9).

In all these personal messages there is only one that suggests a criticism, and it takes the form of a gentle urging. Paul reminds Archippus that he should complete the work God has given to him (4:17). The letter to Philemon is addressed to Archippus also. Paul calls him a "fellow-soldier" and says that there is a church which meets in his home. Surely a soldier who received such encouragement from the apostle Paul himself would finish the battle.

Many think the expression "by my own hand" in verse 18 implies that Paul signed this letter after possibly dictating it, and that he didn't usually sign by hand. Paul makes the one plea for himself, "Remember my chains." Then he closes with the best possible benediction: "Grace be with you."

I pray that God's Word will continue to bear fruit in your life and in the lives of those with whom you come in contact. May the fullness of Christ bring you to complete maturity.

The final chapter will be a review to help you remember what you have learned.

Questions

1. Who did Jesus say is the greatest (Matthew 20:20-28)?
2. What kind of judge is the Lord (2 Timothy 4:8)?
3. When did God first tell man to work (Genesis 2:15)?
4. After man fell, why do you think God increased his work load (Genesis 3:17)?
5. Write what prayer means to you, including your thoughts and actions while praying. Describe your feelings as you pray, believing that God hears each kind of prayer you breathe—a prayer of praise, petition, or simply partaking; of appreciation, invocation or intercession; a prayer of confession, confiding or consecration; of listening, learning or leaning.
6. List names of Christians and the things they do for you.
7. Write a description of Christian maturity. Then compare it to the one you wrote after studying chapter 1.

Chapter 13

Review

Congratulations for your work in learning Christ as He is presented in Paul's letter to the Colossians. If you follow this knowledge with a study of the letter to the Ephesians, your understanding of both books will be enhanced.

If you answer the following questions, all that you have learned will be further impressed in your memory. Finding the answers in your own Bible will help you become familiar with the location of each reference.

1. Who wrote the letter to the Colossians (1:1)?
2. What three things did the Colossians have which impressed Paul favorably (1:4-5)?
3. What had they heard (1:5)?
4. What did Paul ask God for on behalf of the Colossians (1:9)?
5. Why did Paul want them to know God's will (1:10)?
6. What three things has God done for believers (1:12-13)?
7. List eleven statements that tell who Christ is (1:14-22).
8. List ten things that God has done through Christ (1:14-22).
9. What must Christians do in order to be presented holy to God (1:22-23)?
10. What was the mystery Paul made known to these saints (1:26-27)?
11. What hope does this mystery give Christians (1:27)?
12. What is hidden, or stored, in Christ (2:3)?
13. Where are Christians spiritually (2:6-7)?
14. What is the basic error in philosophies of men (2:8)?
15. What dwells in Christ (2:9)? How does this dwell in Him?

16. Where are believers made full (2:10)?
17. Who performs spiritual circumcision on Christians (2:11)?
18. In whose work do Christians have faith (2:12)?
19. In what specific work do Christians have faith (2:12)?
20. On what occasion were believers buried with Christ (2:12)?
21. What was the condition of everyone before they were united with Christ (2:13)?
22. With whom are believers made alive (2:13)?
23. How did Christ cancel our guilt of breaking the law (2:14)?
24. What did the cross do to principalities and powers (2:15)?
25. What was the observance of festivals, new moons and sabbaths (2:16-17)?
26. What caused the false teachers to be "puffed up" (2:18)?
27. What causes people to believe what is untrue (2:19)?
28. To what is the church compared (2:19)?
29. Who maintains and holds the church together (2:19)?
30. Why don't Christians have to live according to man-made religious rituals and rules (2:20)?
31. What did the false teachers tell the Colossian Christians to do and not to do (2:16-18, 21-22)?
32. What kinds of things are useless in guarding against one's fleshly nature (2:23)?
33. What should people who have the new life be most interested in (3:1-2)?
34. Where is Christ now (3:1)?
35. Where is a Christian's old, dead nature (3:3)?
36. What is Christ to Christians (3:4)?
37. What things should Christians make ineffective in their lives (3:5, 8-9)?
38. What will happen to disobedient people (3:6)?
39. What do Christians do when they are baptized (3:9-10)?
40. What classes of people have unity in Christ (3:11)?
41. What are the characteristics of Christians (3:12-14)?
42. What should rule the hearts of Christians (3:15)?
43. What should Christians know well (3:16)?
44. How many of a Christian's activities should be done with the awareness that he belongs to Christ (3:17)?
45. What attitude should wives have toward husbands (3:18)?

46. What attitude should husbands have toward wives (3:19)?
47. Why should children obey their parents (3:20)?
48. What can cause children to become discouraged (3:21)?
49. Who is everyone's Master (3:23-24; 4:1)?
50. For what should Christians pray (4:2-4)?
51. How should Christians behave and speak before non-Christians (4:5-6)?
52. Who delivered this letter to Colosse (4:7-9)?
53. Name three Jewish Christians who were with Paul (4:10-11).
54. Which of Paul's companions were from Colosse (4:9, 12)?
55. Which of Paul's companions wrote books of the New Testament (4:10, 14)?
56. Which of Paul's companions did not remain faithful (4:14)?
57. What other church was to read this letter (4:16)?
58. Who gave Archippus his ministry (4:17)?
59. Where was Paul when he wrote this letter (4:18)?
60. List the ways in which the study of Paul's letter to the Colossians has changed your life.

We pray that we will allow our Hope of Glory to fully become our All in All.

Endnotes

Chapter 1
1. Earl C. Smith, *Paul's Gospel* (Greenwich, N.Y.: Greenwich Book, 1960), 82.
2. Information on gnosticism taken from:
   William Barclay, *The All-Sufficient Christ* (Philadelphia: Westminster, 1963).
   Alexander McClaren, *The Expositor's Bible, Vol. 6* (Grand Rapids, Mich.: Eerdmans, 1943), 191-192.
   Kenneth Wuest, *Word Studies in the Greek New Testament, Vol. I—Colossians* (Grand Rapids, Mich.: Eerdmans, 1973), 163-169.

Chapter 2
1. Wuest, 173.
2. G. G. Findlay, *The Pulpit Commentary, Vol. 20* (Grand Rapids, Mich.: Eerdmans, 1961), 4.
3. John A. Witmer, *Bible Knowledge, Vol. VII* (Wheaton, Ill.: Scripture Press, 1958), 177.
4. McClaren, 200.

Chapter 3
1. Henrietta Mears, *What the Bible Is All About* (Glendale, Calif.: Gospel Light, 1972), 519.
2. H. L. Olmstead, "Know Your Bible—Gospel of John," WHIN radio broadcast (Gallatin, Tenn.), 20 June 1949.
3. Witmer, 170.

4. W. E. Vine, *An Expository Dictionary of New Testament Words* (Old Tappan, N.J.: Revell, 1966), 88.
5. Findlay, 8.
6. Bob Hendren, *Chosen for Riches* (Austin, Texas: Sweet, 1978), 30.
7. Dennis Allen, "The Body—Christ in the World Today," *Word and Work*, Feb. 1980, 50.
8. H. C. Moule, *Studies in Colossians* (Grand Rapids, Mich.: Kregel, 1977), 82.

Chapter 4
1. Smith, 80.
2. Barclay, 71.
3. Moule, 74.
4. Wuest, 180.
5. Moule, 78.
6. Witmer, 171.
7. Hendren, *Chosen for Riches*, 45.

Chapter 5
1. James Strong, *Dictionary of Words in the Hebrew Bible*, word number 5397 (Nashville: Abingdon, 1976), 81.
2. W. Ian Thomas, *The Mystery of Godliness* (Grand Rapids, Mich.: Zondervan, 1964), 71.
3. Ibid., 74.
4. Barclay.

Chapter 6
1. McClaren, 230.
2. H. L. Olmstead, "Know Your Bible—1 John," WHIN radio broadcast (Gallatin, Tenn.), 1950.
3. Moule, 97.

Chapter 7
1. G. Campbell Morgan, *Living Messages of the Books of the Bible* (New York: Revell, 1912), 210-211.
2. Ibid., 210.

3. Bob Hendren, *Sola Gratia* (Dallas: Alternative, 1979), 7 (condensed).
4. Ibid., 7.
5. James Strong, *Dictionary of Words in the Greek New Testament*, word number 907 (Nashville: Abingdon, 1976), 18.
6. C. S. Lewis, *Mere Christianity* (New York: Macmillan, 1960), 175.

Chapter 8
1. R. H. Boll, "A Fatal Oversight," *Word and Work*, reprint Nov. 1968, 329.
2. Vine, 191.
3. Moule, 112.
4. Dennis Allen, "The Body—Walking Together," *Word and Work*, March 1980, 74.

Chapter 9
1. Moule, 120.
2. Strong, *Dictionary of Words in the Greek New Testament*, word number 4202, 59.
3. Mears, 528.

Chapter 10
1. *NIV Study Bible*, footnotes (Grand Rapids, Mich.: Zondervan, 1985), 1798.
2. Strong, *Dictionary of Words in the Greek New Testament*, words 25 and 40, 7.
3. Moule, 127.

Chapter 11
1. Moule, 131.

Chapter 12
1. McClaren, 277.